COVER GIRL

A Photographer's Memoir of a Prized Model

BY MICHAEL STYCKET

Trilogy Christian Publishers
A Wholly Owned Subsidiary of Trinity Broadcasting Network
2442 Michelle Drive
Tustin, CA 92780
Copyright © 2024 by Michael Stycket

Scripture quotations marked ABPE are taken from Aramaic Bible in Plain English, 2010 Copyright©, Rev. David Bauscher, Lulu Enterprises Incorporated, 2010. Scripture quotations marked AMPC are taken from the Amplified Bible, Copyright © 1954, 1958, 1962, 1964, 1965, 1987 by The Lockman Foundation. Used by permission. Scripture quotations marked "BSB" are taken from The Holy Bible, Berean Study Bible, BSB. Copyright ©2016, 2018 by Bible Hub. Used by Permission. All Rights Reserved Worldwide. www.berean.bible. Scripture quotations marked CEV are taken from the Contemporary English Version®. Copyright © 1995 American Bible Society. All rights reserved. Scripture quotations marked ESV are taken from the ESV® Bible (The Holy Bible, English Standard Version®), copyright © 2001 by Crossway Bibles, a publishing ministry of Good News Publishers. Used by permission. All rights reserved. Scripture quotations marked GNT are taken from the Good News Translation® (Today's English Version, Second Edition). Copyright © 1982 American Bible Society. All rights reserved. Scripture quotations marked (LSB®) are taken from the Legacy Standard Bible®, Copyright © 2021 by The Lockman Foundation. Used by permission. All rights reserved. Managed in partnership with Three Sixteen Publishing Inc. LSBible.org and 316publishing.com. Scripture quotations marked MEV are taken from the Modern English Version. Copyright © 2014 by Military Bible Association. Used by permission. All rights reserved. Scripture quotations marked NASB are taken from the New American Standard Bible® (NASB), Copyright © 1960, 1962, 1963, 1968, 1971, 1972, 1973, 1975, 1977, 1995 by The Lockman Foundation. Used by permission. www.Lockman.org. Scripture quotations marked NIV are taken from the Holy Bible, New International Version®, NIV®. Copyright © 1973, 1978, 1984, 2011 by Biblica, Inc. TM Used by permission of Zondervan. All rights reserved worldwide. www.zondervan.com. The "NIV" and "New International Version" are trademarks registered in the United States Patent and Trademark Office by Biblica, Inc.TM. Scripture quotations marked NLT are taken from the Holy Bible, New Living Translation, copyright © 1996, 2004, 2015 by Tyndale House Foundation. Used by permission of Tyndale House Publishers, Inc., Carol Stream, Illinois 60188. All rights reserved. Scripture quotations marked NKJV are taken from the New King James Version®. Copyright © 1982 by Thomas Nelson. Used by permission. All rights reserved. Scripture quotations marked KJV are taken from the King James Version of the Bible. Public domain.

All rights reserved, including the right to reproduce this book or portions thereof in any form whatsoever. For information, address Trilogy Christian Publishing
Rights Department, 2442 Michelle Drive, Tustin, Ca 92780.
Trilogy Christian Publishing/ TBN and colophon are trademarks of Trinity Broadcasting Network.
For information about special discounts for bulk purchases, please contact Trilogy Christian Publishing.

Trilogy Disclaimer: The views and content expressed in this book are those of the author and may not necessarily reflect the views and doctrine of Trilogy Christian Publishing or the Trinity Broadcasting Network.

Cover design created with assets from Freepik and Vectorstock

10 9 8 7 6 5 4 3 2 1
Library of Congress Cataloging-in-Publication Data is available.
ISBN 979-8-89333-159-2
ISBN 979-8-89333-160-8 (ebook)

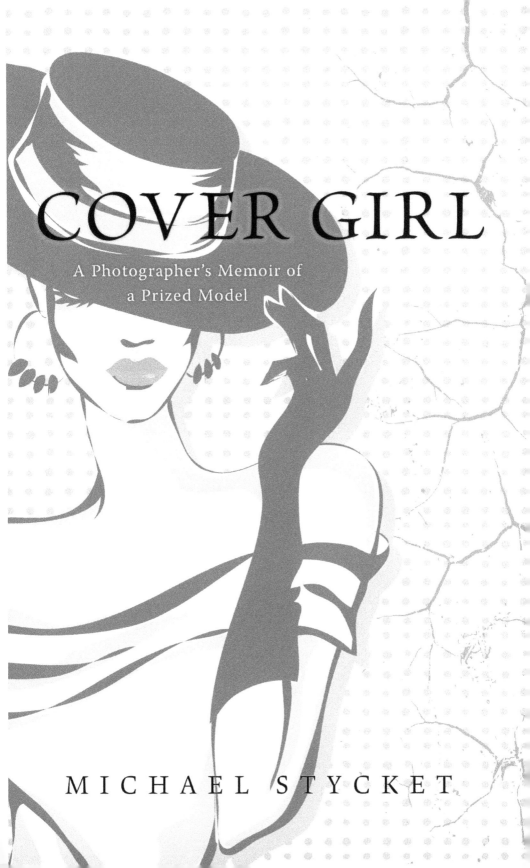

Endorsement

Michael takes us on a riveting spiritual roller coaster ride that isn't pleasant, but it's honest, revealing, and transforming. Rather than wallowing in sorrow and praying for the restoration of what was lost, he bravely looks inward and upward, allowing our God to direct his steps and reveal Himself more through heartbreak.

God can use any of our circumstances or "activating events" to inspire a closer journey with Him, but in this case, it was the loss of Michael's beloved pet and betrayal from the one he hoped would be his forever love. It is inspiring to watch him learn and grow in these pages, caring more about standing "right" before God than looking right before men and women. And the way he writes feels like a cliffhanger lingers at the end of each chapter. The reader can't wait to find out the end of the story with the "Cover Girl."

—Lori Pasion-Gonzales, PhD

Psychologist, California

Table of Contents

Preface ix

Introduction xiii

    Chapter 1: Aslan 1

    Chapter 2: Pin-Up 9

    Chapter 3: Worrying 32

    Chapter 4: Suffering 53

    Chapter 5: Holiday 78

    Chapter 6: Worship 96

    Chapter 7: Good 108

    Chapter 8: Trust 120

    Chapter 9: Forgiveness 134

    Chapter 10: Giving 145

    Chapter 11: Spouse 163

    Chapter 12: Soulmate 184

    Chapter 13: Excellence 200

    Chapter 14: Kira 218

Conclusion 225

Preface

"Blessed are those who find wisdom, those who gain understanding" (Proverbs 3:13, NIV).

This book is a culmination of practical and spiritual lessons learned over time that developed through painful personal growth. These secrets are lessons learned from actual experiences. Truth is not my enemy—it is the enemy of my solution to the ineffable, troubled, throbbing heart alive inside the most vivid, intimate story of my recent past. I lived through it, and now I'm sharing it with those who need it most.

This is for those who are hurting and brokenhearted from the pain of personal hardship and loss. If you are lonely or worried, I hope my story will encourage and guide you. If you have suffered through betrayal and deception, we share a common history. If you have experienced mistreatment or injustice, I hope that you find comfort in the words on these pages. If you have lost a cherished pet or loved one, this will uplift your soul and tug at your heart. If you have gone through rejection or a breakup, you have come to the right place. If you have lingering unforgiveness or distrust with no reason to be generous, you'll find understanding answers here. These and other common evils prevalent in our society today are a result of self-centeredness—of others and our own doing—but all is not lost.

The solutions to these problems are things I discovered and revealed in this book.

Most of my adult professional life has involved working with thousands of eighteen-to thirty-eight-year-old women in the modeling industry. Asking questions and genuine listening became a normal part of this lifestyle for me. This unique experience provided expert insight, perspective, and material for this audience.

I must admit, I am much more comfortable talking to women than I am with men. I am more confident and at ease when addressing a room full of beautiful, intelligent women than one lowly gentleman over a drink. I developed that confident assuredness with women early on. I approached pretty girls about taking their pictures during my senior year in college and learned about women from those conversations like it was my major. This revelation is perhaps why my message is most relevant for adult women and jaw-dropping for men who want to know how women think.

I own several computers, but I drafted the entire contents of this book on an iPhone to prove to myself that I could, with or without a computer, before transferring the manuscript onto my desktop. There's no excuse to do the unusual, and this book is evidence of that. If you want to say something meaningful, the ability to do so is right in the palm of your hand.

I did not have a fierce urge to reexperience in my mind or body the throbbing heart alive inside the most vivid stories from my past. In writing *Cover Girl*, I had no desire to knock myself out emotionally. Memoir may be like therapy for some, but for me, it was often torturous moments of heartbreak while recounting history. I had no desire to go back in time or return to intimate, real feelings I had tried to suppress. I was trying to heal rather than record in detail intense emotional memories. I did not want to miss the geography or atmosphere of heartrending events nor wade deep enough into memory's waters to drown a little, yet I pressed on to reveal the truth and unveil its unsettling storyline and landscape. I liken that yielding moment of decision to "circus clowns pouring out of a miniature trunk, wondering how so much could fit into such a small space?" as Mary Karr would say. Exposing the soft underbelly of my story may offer an emotional connection with you, but for me, it is the spiritual bridge I extend to conjure a longing within for truth and hope.

My examined life and experiences, especially those over five years with a favored Cover Girl, share a raw yet wholesome viewpoint from an unlikely source, a model photographer with some degree of perceived moral bankruptcy. If I err in any recounting, I do so on the side of generosity. I use fairness with honesty toward all characters from my story in hopes of living up to Karr's standards for a memoir. Through my writing, I greeted emotional and physical hardships with open arms. I knew God was using those circumstances to teach me empathy and improve the quality of this publication for you, the reader. I hope it will exceed your expectations.

Some of the events I share in this book are gripping revelations from months or years past. These are not recollections to conjure up drama from love gained then lost long ago. They exist to share suggestions for healing from and prevention of heartbreak. I take you on a journey of emotional thralls so you can experience them with me as close to my heart as it felt in real time. I did not choose this topic or course—it chose me. Writing while going through the issues I share motivated me to help others. It also qualified me with the firsthand experience needed to serve others best. At a time when the whole world is suffering, this subject matter comes to you with the utmost relevance and need.

At its onset, I never intended to share this book, let alone sell it to others. It was more of a method of keeping track of time-tried lessons learned from personal experience. I took copious notes from sermons of respected Christian ministers who added insight and wisdom to my path. I found the need for careful study of the Bible as well. And I also learned that I had to be willing to share my life-long lessons with you so that you could go on the journey with me.

All the chapter titles are one word and each subtitle three, keeping it simple. A broken mind and spirit need order and organization, not confusion and disarray. In my experience, healing from a broken heart also requires hope. I've come to learn the definition of hope is positive anticipation and a desire that something good will happen for you soon. It believes in a happy ending. I trust that will be the case for you while reading my story.

> "Listen to advice and accept instruction, that you may gain wisdom in the future" (Proverbs 19:20, ESV).

Introduction

"Teaching them to observe all that I commanded you…" (Matthew 28:20, NASB1995).

Our story starts on an optimistic January day—a date that will live in infamy in my heart and mind. I missed the call. Her voicemail message said, "I love you. I need you in my life and miss you! I understand if you are hurting and upset." It would be the last time I would hear her voice for months. A couple of weeks later, I saw a video posted on her social media. You know the kind—rose petals led to her bathtub, forming a heart, topped off with a caption gushing about how romantic it was. The only problem was the post had nothing to do with me. And yet, it had everything to do with me. Have you ever had your heart ripped from your chest and diced up into pieces? Have you ever had your hopes vanish in the wind? Have you ever had your dreams stepped on, kicked out of the way, tossed in the trash, then dumped without regard?

I experienced all that and then some. Now, it would be up to me to have to deal with this moving forward. I had never felt so heartbroken in my life. I began to question: Had I ignored the signs? Had I made poor choice after poor choice to lead me here? Had I neglected myself, my heart, and God's leading? The answer was *yes*. But once I realized that truth, I was on my journey to healing with God's guidance and your vicarious observation. How I handle what happens because of her becomes like chicken soup for the brokenhearted. And I intend that the healing powers lining the chapters that follow will be like medicine for your broken heart.

For some reason or another, brokenness and poor choices hid the truth from me—until now. Even worse, I was missing all the visible road signs warning me of and pointing past my bad decisions. This neglect or ignorance was only compounding my problem. So, before we start, I need to share something of paramount importance. I need your commitment not only to read but to consider the time-tested principles in this book. Knowledge puffs up, but godly wisdom put into action produces results. Without allegiance to these revelations, my broken heart may have continued a downward spiral.

The world says, "Listen to me. I have some suggestions for you." But what the world had neglected to tell me is that God has the straightforward truth.

And He says, "Trust Me. I have all the healing answers." It was time for me to crawl out of the dark and reach for the light of truth, wisdom, and joy. This battle is a war of the brokenhearted against the evil principalities of this world, and I invite you to join me in dedication to the mission.

Some of what you read may contradict your beliefs. It may challenge sound logic or seem absurd. But later, you will understand the glorious wisdom behind its results. As I applied the comforting truths inspired by God, I knew they were what the Great Physician ordered. As I practiced them, they healed my heart, restored my broken spirit, and made me whole again. If you need a diversion from the encompassing sorrow, an unexpected twist will fascinate you. I hope you enjoy the mystery of trying to figure it out along the way.

INTRODUCTION

The concepts and stories documented in the pages that follow will guide and stir your heart and mind. They may challenge you to take unusual steps or measures as they did for me, for this is an action book. They will dare you, as they did me, to do things that may seem hard, nonsensical, or a waste of time at first. You may feel that you are getting nowhere in the beginning, exactly like me. If it were easy, everyone would do it. But if you press on and practice some of the principles in this book, I promise that you will one day say, "Now I get it!" That lightning-bolt moment will begin your transition from despair to healing and understanding. Even if you put into action only a few of the gems that I discovered and that I share through my story, you will experience many breakthroughs along the way. Take in the magic oxytocin potion of wisdom lined in the chapters of this book. As you read how they healed me, use them to guide you out of your brokenness.

Much love,

Michael.

"I will instruct you and teach you in the way you should go; I will counsel you with my loving eye on you" (Psalm 32:8, NIV).

CHAPTER 1: ASLAN

"The Lord is close to the brokenhearted and saves those who are crushed in spirit" (Psalm 34:18, NIV).

*I*t was a beautiful spring day in May 2005 as we drove the four hours to Cottonwood, California. Lush green hills under powder-blue skies filled the air with the scent of fresh-cut grass. It tickled our noses, filled our lungs, and increased our excitement. My girlfriend had found a breeder online from whom I could adopt a polydactyl kitten. Having moved here for me eight months earlier, leaving her hometown in South Carolina and flying across the country to surprise me on my birthday, how could I not grant her own heartfelt birthday wish of the cuddly, handpicked, custom kitten? I could not refuse, especially after someone stole our first kitten from my yard only a couple of weeks after we adopted her, devastating my sweetheart. The replacement kitten had to be spectacularly unique to heal her broken heart, even though living in my home, this cat would become my pet.

She fell in love with an orange tabby female with white paws and white fur underneath. Being a special breed, this cat also had functioning thumbs instead of only four little claws. We selected her, and I named her Kira after a beautiful model I had once met. But before we left the breeder, another kitten caught our eyes. It was her brother, who was much bigger than her. Being a polydactyl as well, he had double paws on each front foot, half the width of his head. I was not expecting to adopt two kittens, but we felt compelled to get both brother and sister instead of separating the two. The male looked like a female lion with his tan coloring and green eyes. I named him Aslan, like the lion from the C. S. Lewis book series *The Chronicles of Narnia*. In the books, Aslan represented Jesus and sacrificed himself. Like Jesus, he became the light of my life, confidently roaming my home like he owned the place.

The Kitchen Incident

As a young kitten, Kira smelled something tasty, jumped up onto the counter, and licked a hot pan on the stove with chicken grease simmering in it. I was out of the room only for a few moments. As I reentered the kitchen, she had backed up into a corner near the cupboards. Her jaw swelled up like a little ball almost as big as her face. Her mouth and the tip of her tongue were both burned black. Her two small lower fangs had bent and were ready to fall out of her mouth. I rushed her to the vet, fearing for her life. The doctor gave her a steroid shot and something for the pain, sticking a long needle into her tiny body. Unfortunately, it was too late to save her lower canines and part of her lower lip. Kira's loud, gargled purr was a side effect of the burned mouth and tongue accident. It was an experience that left her cautious and skittish around people other than me for years. It led her to sleep under my arm in bed many a night for the rest of her life. Her brother, Aslan, was much more comfortable around people and very loving. I gave them both lots of attention and love in the different individual ways each needed. "The righteous care for the needs of their animals, but the kindest acts of the wicked are cruel" (Proverbs 12:10, NIV).

Aslan the Entertainer

Aslan had an uncommonly soft purr for such a large cat. He even grew strong enough to pull open the dense, wooden, full-length shutters with one double paw. It amazed many a visitor to my home. In shock, they observed this cat opening something a child would have difficulty opening. Onlookers would marvel at his strength, appearance, and giant paws. Aslan was quite the spectacle and grew to be ever so popular among family, friends, and guests over the years. I always knew when he was up before me in the mornings. I would hear him pulling the shutters open downstairs (so he could watch other animals and birds).

My Constant Companions

On a regular basis, friends or clients would be downstairs in my home. What sounded like children running and jumping around upstairs would thump across the ceiling. It was Aslan chasing his sister up and down the furniture. I cherished and spoiled Aslan like no other animal I had ever known. He and his sister were more than my indoor companions—they were family.

Aslan often spent hours lying on a leather stool behind my desk next to my arm as I worked on the computer. Kira and Aslan played together, slept together, and ate together. They came up and down the stairs together most of the time. Sometimes, when I would wake up in the morning, the first thing I would observe was Kira. She would be sleeping between my legs or under my left arm. Aslan would always be leaning against my left leg. They loved each other and took time grooming each other's coats and faces. They enjoyed looking out the windows together and, of course, chasing one another.

The one difference between them, other than size, was their needs. Kira was always needy and near me at bedtime, falling asleep under my left arm. Aslan was almost always near me during awake hours since I worked from home. And I rarely watched TV on the sofa with my legs up without him wanting to rest his massive body on my lap and legs. I could never pet or brush him enough. He loved his belly rubbed and his whiskers brushed with his special brush. Every morning, I would take the sleepers out of the corners of his eyes and call him my little boy. He often followed me around the house like a puppy, trailing me downstairs for breakfast. At night, he would stay up with me, whether it be till midnight or 2 a.m. He would follow me faster or run ahead of me if I called his name and said, "Come on, boy, come here," or "Let's go to bed!"

Aslan loved me, but he loved his sister more than anything. In late 2017, I sensed that the Lord was telling me that my long time with them was nearing an end. I praised God for them both and asked Him to extend their lives for me. Then, one day in 2018, between the transition of fall into winter, I had left a couple of windows open at night. Being under the covers, I did not realize how cold it got in the house. Kira, being a smaller cat, developed a cough and hack that left me fearing for her health. One morning, Aslan and I watched in concern over her coughing underneath the guest bed. My heart sank as I considered the possibility of Aslan losing his fragile sister. She recovered, though, within days. The playful sounds of them chasing each other around the house soon returned. I thanked the Lord for Aslan and Kira pretty much every morning and night on my knees. Their names were some of the first words in prayer to leave my lips.

An Unexpected Day

I remember one December day a couple of months after Kira's coughing scare. I petted Aslan more than once while rubbing his tummy to endearing purrs of joy before leaving for work that evening. I returned that night to his sister coming downstairs to greet me rather than him, which seemed unusual. I skimmed through my emails on the computer before going upstairs. Before I even had a chance to turn on a light, I noticed Aslan in the dark, lying in my bedroom between my bed and closet. I approached him and called his name. My heart sank with a gripping fear when he did not move.

I fell to my knees in sobbing grief as I petted his lifeless body, saying over and over, "Oh, Aslan, my little boy. I'm so sorry I was not here for you. I love you." I thanked the Lord for all the years with him as I knelt beside him in shock. I had thought we would have a couple more years together. His poor, fragile sister would now have to spend the rest of her life alone. I had lost my most loyal friend and daily companion of fourteen years. I had gone through a very devastating loss the year prior, which developed new habits in me due to hard times.

Without hesitation, from a disciplined routine, I began thanking and praising the Lord. I repeated Psalm 34:18 (NIV): "The LORD is close to the brokenhearted and saves those who are crushed in spirit." I mumbled along with Psalm 147:3 (NIV): "He heals the brokenhearted and binds up their wounds." I cried out loud, Psalm 126:5 (MEV), "Those that sow in tears shall reap in joy." Unfortunately, at that moment, I was not experiencing anything that resembled happiness. I tried focusing on Psalm 56:8 (NLT), "You keep track of all my sorrows. You have collected all my tears in your bottle. You have recorded each one in your book," for comfort.

God had a purpose in allowing me to go through a painful experience the year prior. I was now finally beginning to understand one reason why. He was preparing me for times like this. It led me to memorize, meditate on, and use various Bible verses in daily prayer. Four of those verses immediately came to my mind the moment I found Aslan's lifeless body. Those verses brought solutions that made this book possible and led to the cure for my brokenness and now, perhaps, yours.

It was clear now that I would need the Lord more than ever at this bereft moment of grief and for all the days to follow. I called Jenna, one of my closest friends, and bawled my eyes out, only able to mumble that Aslan had died. She loved Aslan as well and texted me in the middle of the night how she was so distraught that she could not sleep. She was also by my side when we buried Aslan the next day in my backyard, even saying a prayer for me over his grave. I appreciated the Lord providing her support during that time. "Blessed are those who mourn, for they will be comforted" (Matthew 5:4, NIV).

The verses I prayed over my lifeless pet and companion that night were a source of comfort, strength, and healing. They assured me that the Lord was with me at this darkest of moments. You can only call upon the promises of God and His mighty power if you know the Word of God. If it's already committed to memory, you, too, can call upon it in your times of need and brokenness.

The Plane Ride

I finished this chapter to the sounds of a fourteen-month-old baby boy crying and screaming at the top of his tiny lungs. Milk drooled down his face, just inches from me during my flight to Arizona for Christmas. His mother tried to comfort him in the seat to my right. In the meantime, an overweight, middle-aged man to my left awakened from his nap with earphones on. He coughed into my face without a care in the world or any acknowledgment of my presence. Blood-curdling cries from another baby in the aisle next to us was only adding fuel to the fire at this point. I felt compressed like a sardine in this uncomfortable moment, trapped in my brokenness. All these feelings only brought my experience with Aslan to the forefront of my mind. It even reminded me of the verse Job 13:15 (NKJV): "Though He slay me, yet will I trust Him," a verse I would come to repeat in many a prayer. The next moment, the baby next to me hit me in the face with something in his hand, spilling my complimentary juice into my lap.

Meanwhile, the heavy-set man continued to cough without regard as the mother said, "Sorry if he hit you in the eye." She noticed my watery eyes and tears, which were not so much from her son or this broken situation. They were from knowing that God was giving me the grace and ability to go through this nightmare. He helped me while writing about Aslan, hardly noticing the turbulence along the way.

If you have experienced the heartbreak that results from losing a cherished pet, I know your grief. There is no kind of pain worse than emotional pain. In first grade, a car hit me. As a teen, a beach-born sunburn left me bedridden for two days. A high school tackle out of bounds left me with a cracked elbow and palms covered in blood. A rainy day in my mid-twenties sent my vehicle (without airbags or seatbelt) into a parked car at fifty mph, and an injured shoulder prevented me from sleeping on my stomach for six weeks. Over the years, I've had four broken bones and ribs bruised so extreme in football that I couldn't breathe on the way to the hospital. At a younger age than typical, I had shingles on the side of my head for days that Vicodin couldn't soothe. I've had food poisoning, my wisdom teeth pulled, and four accident-related operations. Yet I would take physical pain any day over a broken heart. Your heart might be breaking, but you do not have to break with it. The best way to heal a broken heart is to give God all the pieces. His path leads to the road of healing.

> "You, Lord, hear the desire of the afflicted; you encourage them, and you listen to their cry" (Psalm 10:17, NIV).

CHAPTER 2: PIN-UP

"A wife of noble character who can find? She is worth far more than rubies" (Proverbs 31:10, NIV).

The First Meeting

It was a call like many others over the years—someone who knew me well gave her my number. I knew my LA-based friend usually referred women with potential who wanted to see themselves in print. The woman on the line said she had been a model since college but was never published, which made the reason for her call a familiar one. It was common for women to call me if they wanted to be in a magazine or calendar. She wanted me to photograph her so we could work together—a roundabout way to gain fame via publications. It took a couple of months, but our schedules eventually worked out to meet for lunch this spring 2015 day.

She strode into the room, with the grace of a resplendent supermodel navigating the tables and chairs. Everyone was looking at her. She dazzled onlookers to the sound of Bruno Mars singing "Uptown Funk," Billboard's number-one song at the time, over the loudspeakers. The chatter of customers and silverware clanking among those dining went from deafening to a low rumble as she approached me. Making her way swiftly through the crowd, the sound of her designer boots stepping across the hardwood floor seemed to echo off the ceiling. Her big smile illuminated the dimly lit room like a beacon glowing in the dark. She captivated my senses, overpowering the smell of pizza, burgers, and Alfredo sauce that permeated the restaurant. I was agape at the spectacle of it all—smitten and in awe. She was the makings of star stuff—front row, center of attention, pin-up material, making me the most envied guy in the room.

The packed house at the Lazy Dog restaurant forced us to sit at the bar. It meant that we would sit closer to each other than I would typically do when first meeting someone. With her sitting to my left, much of our conversation came with her turned and facing me. Had I been inexperienced or two decades younger, I might have been fidgeting, tapping my foot repeatedly, and sweating excessively. By now, I'm like Shania Twain with this stuff. "That don't impress me much." My professional routine kicked in, allowing me to push aside the immediate and intense physical attraction which raised my blood pressure that sent a flush of warmth to my forehead and ears. She was good-looking with a capital "G" in my book, and others concurred, given the number of rapt heads that turned, drooling like Pavlov's dogs.

Her outfit was stylish and snug, with a plunging neckline that revealed her cleavage. Her long, wavy, flowing blonde hair shimmering in the light drew eyes to where we sat. Her face was pristine, polished, and wholesome looking. Her sparkling teeth and dazzling eyes were mesmerizing. She was also the first model to ever show up for an interview with me in a cast—a reminder that even magnificent beauty is subject to exquisite fragility. She had informed me earlier that she had broken her hand and the fiberglass would be coming off soon. That was only one of the many caveats that made the meeting memorable.

She fudged a little bit on her age, wanting me to think she was five years younger—a common practice in the business. It was not something I discovered until I needed a copy of her ID months later to publish her. It did not matter—she had the looks and charisma that fit my typical type of work. Thinking she was only twenty-two, like she had written on her model application, I had nothing more than business and friendship on my mind as usual. Yet, there were qualities about her that were compelling—an instantaneous fancy. She also knew how to wheedle into my good graces, then butter up—noting that meeting Michael Stycket was the best thing to ever happen to her—no surprise, given that her aspirations were modeling and acting. But it was all in jest. She was loquacious at first but polite and enthusiastic about everything we discussed. Her voice, fluctuating in pitch and tone, rang like sweet regale music in my typically monotone ears. The intense *simpatico* seemed to blur the others in the room as if they didn't exist. It was like feasting on my favorite pizza after fasting for a week.

We created a stage name for her—Jenna—which went with her wholesome, pious vibe. She seemed to have impeccable character (aside from the age flub), personality, charm, and an extraordinary smile to go with those impressive curves. With no money and all that talent, charging her didn't cross my mind, so I never brought it up. Most models hired me to photograph them over the years, but this was not going to be one of them. Our developing nascent friendship over the phone before meeting made the ease of our interaction natural without the coaxing used by some of my other models. The mutual comfort level over lunch was one of the reasons we became good friends that day. We hit it off well, even sharing our meal and sparkling waters—something we would come to do for years. The meeting ended with an innocent hug initiated by her rather than a handshake. Little did I realize the thunderclap to come.

Our First Photoshoot

I picked up Jenna and her makeup artist bestie from childhood. She plopped into the front seat, shotgun-style, without a hitch like we had done it before.

"I'm so excited, Michael," Jenna exclaimed, bouncing up and down in her seat like we were on our way to ski in Tahoe. The ride to Sacramento from San Jose was full of laughs and fun with the one who would become my frequent copilot and wing-woman. Jenna's giggle alone could wipe the frown off the most "golem" of facial expressions. And oh, that smile. "A woman's smile is her umbrella on a rainy day," wrote Mira Bartók in *The Memory Palace*. The fitness shots we did at the gym came out excellent, but unexpectedly, the picture we took later that day in the hallway of my nephew's home made the calendar's cover. It would be the first of many covers together and the start of an exclusive preternatural working relationship.

Shooting into the evening at my nephew's provided an excellent photo setting and a way to visit family. After a long day, we all finally had dinner together. Since it was getting late and everyone was having fun, we decided to stay and save the long drive home for the next day. It also would give me more time to spend with my young nephews. Her playing and interacting with my nephews caught my eye, but I was already dating someone else at the time. Plus, Jenna was twenty-two, or so I thought, which was too young for me. She fit in well with everyone and drew plenty of attention. This first shooting experience would be the makings of a long and loyal friendship. That night left me with my youngest nephew in one room and the giggling girls in another.

The next day, on the ride home, I drove to a Starbucks, where I showed the girls a couple of magic tricks with a deck of cards. It was only an excuse to banter and get another giggle out of Jenna, my newfound sidekick wing-woman. Over time, our friendship grew as we stayed in touch weekly, which led to our next big adventure.

The Girlfriend Shoot

It was early summer that year when I invited Jenna to join two other models (one being my girlfriend) and me for another road trip. This one would be to Monterey, California, where a friend let me use his mansion to do photoshoots for a season. He got to meet pretty girls each month while the models took exquisite location shots. The pictures resulted in many published works, which was the models' endgame. This trip presented some unexpected complications, though. I thought Jenna, as my new sidekick, getting to meet and shoot with my girlfriend, who was also a model, would be a fun idea. Fat chance. From the moment my girlfriend took the front seat from Jenna, I realized my error. What was I thinking? It was a blunder imagining my girlfriend would get along well with Jenna, my newest favored model. It would be no comedy of wars, and I was as wrong as Kevin Hart was funny.

My tempestuous girlfriend used every opportunity to exude her presumed place of importance and took control of all conversations. Given their similar political views, I could have used their stand on politics to create some amiable conversation—like that ever works. To ease tensions, we stopped at a clothing store along the way, and I bought her something to shoot in, hoping to appease her while giving the women a moment apart. Instead, it only ignited the rivalry, pitting one against the other as my pompous girlfriend led us to opposite ends of the store. The building tension throughout the day was as agonizing as slow-moving fingernails on a chalkboard. I stood as close to my girlfriend as possible without seeming like I was with her, and I stood as far back as I could without leaving the planet.

Upon reaching the mansion, my girlfriend received less attention from its owner, being unavailable and out of respect for me. My brilliant idea of going back and forth, shooting one model, then the other, backfired as well. Shooting this way is standard practice when photographing more than one model individually, but it only fueled the competition in the mansion's dressing room, as I later learned. How did I not see this coming? By midday, my girlfriend and Jenna both hated each other and made sure I knew it. Torn by loyalty in both directions, I was at my wit's end. Thank God I did not foresee that this sprawling banter and rivalry between them would continue long after this day. God, in His humorous way, must realize it is best we do not know the end from the beginning. If we knew what lay ahead, we might shrivel up in fear or become prideful and feel no need for Him.

Two Life-Changing Decisions

Following the shoot and then dinner, the mansion owner pulled Jenna aside and invited her to stay overnight. Not knowing what shady intentions this guy had in coaxing my new exclusive model prodigy, I'm sure I made a face like I was asking Willis what he was talkin' 'bout. She let me know her acceptance of the offer, so we left without her. At that moment, all respect for her and future possibilities lay in the balance. Was I wrong about the character of this person? I felt flummoxed. A few minutes later, she called me, asking

CHAPTER 2: PIN-UP

if we could come back to retrieve her. She told us that when the mansion owner revealed his real intentions were to sleep with her, she immediately declined, thus the call to me.

Then everything went south as if it hadn't already. My capricious girlfriend had an insufferable fit when we turned around to get the person she had come to despise. With varying inflections in her voice, she called her every evil name in the dirty little book of slanderous, callous condemnations. Her comments and attitude revealed a selfish and heartless side I was only starting to see now. (We had only been dating six months after being set up by a good friend.) Simultaneously, with respect for my wing-woman restored, our destiny changed in a mainspring way neither of us could know.

On the drive home, my girlfriend got steely silent—the kind of internal quiet that makes others nervous when they see you go there because it means you're stewing and plotting. Then, attack mode set in, and my girlfriend's berated treatment of Jenna went from cold to downright disrespectful. At Jenna's request, I assured her that I would stop at a store so she could get an energy drink before driving home so late from my place. My girlfriend would have no part of it, wanting me to drop her off if we stopped so she could get an Uber back home—so I did. Exiting the car and grabbing her bag out of the trunk, she made sure to leave Jenna with one last piece of her mind—the "B" word. It left me with a choice. That scene left a bitter aftertaste in my mouth, so I chose the friendship of my wing-woman over the relationship with my girlfriend, whose hyperbole was wrong. That life-changing decision was the only choice a gentleman could make, and so I did, for I could see the tip of an insurmountable damaged iceberg. That overblown pettifoggery was the beginning of the end with that girlfriend and a surefire start of solidifying loyalty between Jenna and me.

Calendars and Magazines

Jenna and I genuinely enjoyed each other's company. And that's because she's the kind of present you get from someplace good, like Tiffany & Co. or Prada. All I wanted was to unwrap her thoughts and admire her sparkle and quality features. In return, I dazzled her with the glitter and glamour of beautiful, published photos of herself. Many magazine and calendar shootings of Jenna, ending in platonic, fun-filled dinner conversations, followed that night. I hate to admit that I did not break it off with my girlfriend for quite a few months after her bad behavior. But God knows the end of our story from the beginning, for that decision kept me unavailable. It also kept both women at odds, strengthening the growing innocent relationship with Jenna.

"What do you see in her?" and "You could do so much better than her!" were typical expressions of Jenna's frustration.

My little nephew, having met both women, even asked me the same questions. By the time my girlfriend and I were no longer a couple, Jenna was now pretty much my best friend. I photographed her on the beach, at gyms, in multi-million-dollar homes, by pools, and at my studio. Many meals together and heart-filled, thought-provoking conversations followed more shootings and publications. I was indulging her with lavished plenitude while creating my own fandom experience. By our second shared Christmas, I presented my spoiled sidekick with a gift of remembrance. It was a leather-bound portfolio filled with pages of her published covers we had shot together. Each page was a different calendar or magazine cover of her in various outfits—pin-up material for any male with hormones. Wrapping it in a custom red Cover Model T-shirt and Cover Model baseball cap topped off the surprise with the appropriate attire for a Cover Girl—an outfit that said Cover Model. The gifts were part of a package she labeled as the most meaningful she had ever received. Friendship led to lots of time together that no longer required a magazine shoot, another calendar, or talk of such. We continued to shoot together only because she loved and requested it.

The Wedding Realization

I informed Jenna that my sister was getting married in Laguna Beach in only a few months. With a big smile and giggle, her response blurted out our destiny.

"I'll be your plus-one!" Jenna said with confident assurance.

I had no idea at the time, but I was hopelessly committed to this relationship at that unsuspecting tender moment. Behind those dazzling eyes and batting lashes was a secret agenda of how things were going to be. It had only taken me a year from our very first meal together to get to this point. I believed that the inside of this person represented a place where I could find permanent rest. There were things about her I could not replace with someone else. In all His humorous ways, God showed once again that He knows the end from the beginning.

The day of our long drive came the day following my plus-one posing for a bridal magazine cover in Las Vegas, where we met at the Hard Rock Hotel after her shoot. We drove from Vegas to Laguna Beach, where we grabbed dinner and a hotel room in a city near the wedding location. We rested in separate beds, sharing the same room.

On the morning of the wedding, I found myself gazing at Jenna doing her makeup in the hotel mirror. All dressed from the waist down, with only a bra on top, confusion started unfolding within me. I'd seen her this way, preparing for photoshoots, but never before did it feel like a date. Turning away, I was a flutter of confusing emotions springing up inside. I brushed it off and refused to ponder these thoughts, forcing myself to interact with her as usual.

Later, over breakfast at Mimi's Café, I could feel my heart ready to burst out of my chest. She reached for her water, and her eyes sparkled before she said, "I just want someone to love and adore me."

If she only knew! I wanted to shout, "Look! He's right in front of you." I was screaming in my mind! But instead, I said nothing. It took every ounce of control not to spew the scrambled eggs and bacon I was miserably trying to force down. It was too early. I'd prefer to say that I had to trust that God's way was perfect and that His plan would unfold in His perfect timing. The truth was, I did not want to jeopardize any part of our relationship by jumping the gun.

Later that day, after my sister's sunset wedding on the beach, Jenna and I fast danced for the first time during the reception. Her bounce, sway, and agility in perfect motion to the beat of the music left me captured, mesmerized, and enthralled by the moment. I was in awe. Then I recalled her telling me that she had been a cheerleader in high school who went on to do state completions. *Wow*, I thought, admiring her precision and moves. She must have been a showstopper, for my heart was a flutter as when my high school crush, also a cheerleader, first kissed me in public, communicating that she wanted to be my girlfriend. Like swiftly falling dominos, my affection for Jenna changed on a dime that day—leaving an indelible mark on my brain. What an unexpected wedding realization this had been.

Shopping and Shooting

I planned an exclusive shoot for Jenna in a San Francisco home owned by a friend. So what do you do when you spoil an exceptional woman before her shoot? You got it—you take her shopping. And I had a heart for extravagance when it came to Jenna. I enjoyed indulging her in a way my sister—my greatest confidante—would have frowned upon, for I drew a hard line on anything that seemed to waste money on myself.

So, how did our no-holds-barred shopping spree go? First, we went to a department store where Jenna tried on some of her favorites, with a few helpful suggestions from me of course. I got her whatever she wanted—it all looked alpha-girl stunning on her. The next stop was the store that is a bore for most men, but near and dear to many American women. Victoria's Secret had a few necessities that would be useful, so I got Jenna a few more items she selected. Waiting among the various shades of pink and hexadecimal red colors and sweet-smelling perfumes, I enjoyed Jenna calling me to the dressing room to see her choices. My heart pounded and palms moistened with every moment of anticipating the next change in her attire. I had done similar a thousand times as a routine with models at my studio with little fanfare or emotion. This was different. Our third stop was Nordstrom, where she selected a couple of pairs of shoes and did an adorable dance holding tennis shoes while I recorded her. Jenna giggled the whole way through what she was good at (dancing) while doing what she loved (shopping) for something she held dear (modeling the latest styles). Fashion was her passion, and I had a trained eye for it.

One week later, before we headed to the City, I took Jenna to MAC, where they beautified her soft white skin so that her face resembled an angel. Almost all models I shoot get their makeup done by a professional before showing up at my studio. But Jenna was the one exception I spoiled as her chauffeur and stylist. Having a man pamper you this way is something any woman can appreciate. Models who come to me have a plan of some goal they are trying to achieve through their shoot. This shoot of Jenna was different. It was more for us and doing what we loved together for no one else but us.

The remodeled San Francisco relic came alive only because Jenna was the life of the shoot, whose charm and beauty brightened the home like a Roman candle. We took amazing photographs in a room with three sizable old-fashioned windows facing a typical-looking city street. Jenna had a fun time and looked stunning. She photographed so well that it made my studio and natural light work look more professional than usual. Before the shoot ended, we got some marvelous sunset images on a private rooftop overlooking the city and bay. I could have stayed up there for hours shooting her in that tiny red number or the polka dot outfit, but Jenna felt the chill of the cold Bay temperature. Another day of fun with Jenna was in the books. There was a unique closeness brewing between the two of us, which led to the day of asking *the* question.

The Gym Dance

"When did you first realize?" said Jenna with a curious smile.

Without using the complete version of the question, she was inquiring about when I first knew I liked her as more than a friend. Assuming that I had come to this conclusion, her bold trick question was a clever ploy for confirmation. I took the bait without hesitation.

"When I saw you goofing off doing your little dance while working out together today," was my response.

Now she knew. I had been denying my feelings since the wedding breakfast, but no longer. It was the first time I verbalized romantic feelings toward her in words rather than actions. More workouts together, movies, prayer before meals, gift shopping, church, and the joy of being together led to our next adventure.

One of the things Jenna and I would practice with frequency was going to the gym. We rarely exercised together when we got there, but we always dined together after a workout. Her preferred restaurant still provides our favorite red chowder soup and fish tacos. We always shared a single bowl, along with our sparkling mineral water. The one time they served us two cups instead of one bowl to share, it was not as good.

"It just doesn't taste the same," were her exact words.

She also introduced me to Thai food for the first time, and life was never the same. I would tell her the American version of what I liked, and she would order the Thai version for me—I loved it. It also became a frequent cuisine for us, but it all started with the gym workout.

The Ariana Experience

We enjoyed exercising together, but I loved talking with Jenna and listening to her cheerful voice. I snapped to attention when I saw her face light up my phone screen. I spent weeks in reverie, daydreaming about the next time she would call or text to inform me that she would be in town that weekend and wanted to stay over. I was rapt and flattered that my prized pin-up had come to a mindset of craving addiction to be in my presence. I mean, she was so adorable in personality and so good-looking. I was agog with her intentions for our evenings and marveled at the clarity and sparkle in her eyes each time we stood or sat face to face like I was ogling a precious gem. They drove me bananas and coconuts. So, I took the initiative on my own this time.

It was spring, and I texted Jenna from out of town. "I am back home from Vegas for the Ariana Grande concert on the 27th. I do not want to take another girl and get her hopes up. I want to take the person who cracks me up when she dances. Not for the music but for the fun and laughter we have together. You know who that person is!"

Jenna's response revealed her typical presumption and confidence: "Me!"

We arranged the details, and that was that.

On the day of the event, following our workout and lunch, I took her to the mall and her favorite women's clothing store. Walking in, I told her she could pick out anything she wanted to wear at the concert, and I would get it for her. I'd done this before with her, but most of those gifts were for shooting. We went through the outfits, dresses, accessories, and more. I went from rack to rack, pulled down contenders, and handed them to her for consideration. An eye for exceptional taste in women's apparel excelled from years of photographing women. Once she had everything chosen (with a few of my suggestions, out of habit from helping models make such decisions and enhance Jenna's experience), we were off to my studio with a joyful skip in our steps so Jenna could change into her new outfit.

After freshening up, Jenna went downstairs, where my best makeup artist was waiting. She sat, giggling and beaming like a whimsical teen, on the fancy stool, surrounded by professional makeup. Being primed and pampered for an hour was not unusual. I had done this for her several times before, but never for the sole purpose of a night out. Once perfected—and boy, was she dolled up—she asked me to do a few shots of her in the studio before we left, so I did.

Before the concert, we stopped off at Scott's Seafood. Scott's was upscale and elegant, and to get in, you had to book a reservation several weeks prior. My heart pounded in excitement as we rode up the restaurant elevator together as I thought of what I was concealing. I had a little surprise for her. Jenna grabbed onto my arm and sighed at the opening elevator doors. As we walked into the entry, the woman at the podium immediately greeted us with smiles and professional courtesy, with a nod to acknowledge Jenna's posh attire and make-up to perfection. From there, she escorted us to the dining area that had a long window stretching across the left side. The breathtaking view of the city lights below and the buildings in the background was spectacular from this vantage point. My heart raced with excitement during this romantic scene as Jenna's smile gleamed after taking in the view and our seating location.

Our table had a perfect city view, not so much from my request but because she looked like a Cover Girl. Everything was fancy, including the white tablecloth and elevated spot on the floor. Our sparkling silverware and china were the perfection of class. While I sat to her right, Jenna looked stunning—a candle-fragrant beauty, as she faced the best view in the house. Our *maître d'* was charming and so professional. Watching Jenna scan our surroundings with a smile and twinkle in her eye, with all the attention focused on her, was precisely the reaction I had hoped to see. It's not in my nature to take the spotlight. I'm the guy who shines it.

Before our meal arrived, I could not hold it in any longer, nor could she. She wanted to know what I was hiding. I placed the box in front of her as her face lit up like Disneyland fireworks on the Fourth of July. This surprise was a moment that came after careful thought and planning.

As she opened the box, she exclaimed, "Oh, Michael. It's beautiful."

She immediately put on the thin gold bracelet so that the cross would connect the two ends and meet on top of her wrist. She would come to wear it every day.

We shared our sumptuous dessert with smiles. Relieved and thrilled that Jenna loved her gift and classy dining experience, we departed for the concert. Upon arriving at the arena, our perfect seating provided a great view of the stage and packed house. I knew most of the words to Ariana's songs, and the concert was fun even though it was not Jenna's favorite music genre. The evening was more about making her happy in the experience of sharing this night. The dinner, more than the concert, reassured me of our connection and my unfolding feelings. It felt like God's plan, although who was I to say what the Lord had in store? A lot more dinners, stay-overs in my guestroom, and me cooking her favorite breakfast then led to the big day.

Meeting the Parents

That morning, I got a text from Jenna that read, "Today's the Big Day!"

Reading those assuring words of excitement confirmed she was on board with us moving forward in our relationship. She was referring to the long-awaited big day of meeting her parents, and I wondered how long she would stay my wing-woman. How much longer until she could be more? To say I was nervous and excited was the understatement of the century.

"What do I wear?" I asked.

"Something stylish, like you always do," was her response.

I was a bundle of nerves with a sweaty brow and thumping chest most of the hour-long drive to their home. I had fallen for a girl whose parents were not that much older than me. I also knew from Jenna that her dad was a hard one to win over. It would be even more difficult given that I photographed scantily dressed women for a living. I had been to their home before to pick up or drop off my sidekick but had never met the parents until this day. This time was different. It signified that I was now under consideration as more than a photographer or a good friend, which was what I wanted. I was now a potential suitor of their prized daughter, and our fate lay in their approval. I wanted to make a good impression. Once in her hometown, I stopped at a gas station bathroom along the way to pause and catch my breath. My curious and protective sister kept texting me, being almost as nervous and anxious as I was. Family impressions always matter, and I wanted Jenna's family to know that my intentions were pure and true. I had their daughter's best interest at heart, and I would not lay a romantic hand on her without their approval.

I could feel my heart thump with each of my three knocks on the door. Jenna was quick to greet me at the front door, all smiles as usual. Moving down the short hallway to the living room felt like walking in waist-high water. I was as nervous as a teenager on a first date. Her gracious mom rose from her seat, hugged me, and treated me like a long-lost son, making me feel loved and at home. I was less sure about Jenna's father, who was reserved and quiet, making them complete opposites. He sat on the sofa, relaxing, his baseball cap mounted and the Giants' game on the widescreen dominating most of his attention. He appeared cautious and laid back, and I was unsure of his blessing upon our blossoming romance.

I find it easier to read women than men, which did not help any this day. Trying to hide any diffidence, I reached for and received her father's handshake. Most of the small talk was between Jenna's mom and me while I waited for her daughter and clung to her husband's hints of approval. I was part stranger, part friend, in a room of shelves bedecked with all the trappings of family photos and memories from years gone by.

With Jenna in her bedroom getting ready while I chatted with her parents, I received no feedback about whether I measured up in her dad's eyes. My first impression was not so fast. For Jenna was the kind of quintessential princess that knows to la-la-la-la-la-live for today, confident she will always have dad, if not me, to lavish her with the security of high-maintenance attention and pampering. She walked out of her room, dressed more conservative than usual in a turtleneck shirt and long khaki-colored skirt. I was unsure of what this meant, but I knew one thing. It was one more confirmation that this was Dad's cherished daughter, and all the signs were to go slow and steady.

This day was when we first held hands while walking to dinner before going to the theater. I remember two things about holding her hand for the first time. First, it was too soon and may have scared her a little. Second, her palms were surprisingly rough for a woman, unlike the touch of the skin on her face and waistline, which felt thin and frail to the fingertips. Her fingers were long and slender and carried a similar roughness in her grip. I never thought about that before when holding hands in prayer together, but this kind of holding was different. I know it may sound funny, but the texture did not matter to me. I was falling for a person, not a body, nor was I expecting perfection or lasting beauty. It was at this hand-holding moment that I knew with grown-up maturity what matters in attraction to a person—what's on the inside. In either case, Jenna and I now knew our future would consist of more lasting things than modeling or seeking pin-up opportunities.

The Arizona Reveal

The day of Jenna finally meeting my sister in her home had arrived. Jenna met my sister once before at her wedding, but it was too brief for an extended conversation with so many other people attending. A couple of days would make for more meaningful conversation opportunities.

Jenna and I flew together from San Jose to Arizona with her seated on my right side, no different from all the times I drove her in my car. The excitement and anticipation spread further than the wings of the plane. This time it was her moment to be nervous and excited while it was my turn to be confident and assured. After landing, luggage gathered and our Starbucks in hand, we called an Uber and were off.

Our first stop was a Phoenix high-rise penthouse suite for another photoshoot. A friend who let me use his place to take pictures before let me do so again for the day on the way to our stay at my sister's. The spectacular penthouse view of the Phoenix cityscape drifting into distant mountains made for stunning photographic backgrounds. My panache sidekick had a great time as I spoiled her like royalty, hoping to create flawless memories of the multi-million dollar setting. It was like teasing her with glimpses of what a permanent future by my side could resemble. She had no idea I had prepared my whole life to take care of the right woman someday. From early afternoon to sunset, we laughed and had fun at what we did best: taking pictures throughout the penthouse interior and balcony. Working well together was a perfect partnership—but being together was our destiny. Bringing Jenna as my first female of interest to my sister's new home would be confirmation of that bright future. Enthusiasm was high.

After I led Jenna through the estate gate, we approached my sister's front door, flanked by an enclosed corridor of opulent desert plants and neatly placed outdoor décor. My building nervous uncertainty was in check. My sister, a former model herself and now a successful businesswoman, was not swayed by beauty and acting skills like a man can fall prey. Greeting us with hugs reassured me of the warm welcome I had anticipated from my sister since she has my best interest at heart.

She offered us bottled water in the kitchen to the aroma of mouth-watering peppered chicken and fresh garlic bread, and I watched Jenna relax into some amiable conversation. It was a relief to see my sister and Jenna get along as they walked the marble floors of my sister's posh home. Now they would finally have the opportunity and time to get to know one another. I stayed back, greeting my little nephew as my sister gave Jenna a tour of the backyard pool, the rooms, and Jenna's guest room. Hearing their pleasant voices and laughter from the other side of the house gave me hope for an optimistic future.

After the successful shoot and pleasant dinner at my sister's, we all settled in front of the TV for some cozy relaxation time. It had been a long day for Jenna, so she headed off to her room to freshen up, I assumed. Then, everything in our happy little life changed in an instant.

My sister approached me from the hallway, hunched over, and whispered.

"I need to speak with you," she said. The look on her face was stern and concerned.

Suddenly, it dawned on me that the mood was as tense and foreboding as when my prescient sister discovered her ex was seeing one of my previous models—someone my sister had done makeup for on a shoot. That disconcerting experience could have triggered, like a Geiger counter, an instinctive reaction of the accused, tried, and convicted in my sister's court of loyalty and disrespect. I listened with full attention. The tone of my sister's voice conveyed something dreadful, and I felt the fear rush up my spine as I held my breath.

She continued, her voice low and intense. "I overheard a conversation from the guestroom," she explained with anger and disbelief. "Wondering what was going on, I heard enough before I could even knock on the door," she continued in earnest. "There was a guy on the line with Jenna, and it was apparent a romantic relationship is going on between them."

I went from erect in my seat with attention toward my sister's voice as she spoke to me to slumped on the sofa like a deflated inner tube. I now understood the meaning of "when the walls come tumbling down on you" and "pulling the rug out from under your feet." I marinated in utter incredulity for a moment, wondering if Jenna would hide such illicit deception from me.

I wanted to press the reset button this evening and conclude it with a different reality. Knowing my sister would never lie to me, I feared the worst but had to find out the truth for myself. There are always two sides to a story, no matter how sound the evidence. I decided to confront Jenna and give her the opportunity to explain.

I walked toward Jenna's guestroom in disbelief, hoping this was all an innocent misunderstanding. I knocked on the door.

"Jenna?" I tried to keep my voice calm. "Would you join me for a talk?"

She opened the door, looking a little concerned, perhaps interrupted, and followed as I turned.

"What's up?" she asked.

"We just need to talk," I replied in a soft, serious voice.

Caught off guard, she joined me on the backyard sofa for what I assumed would be the heart-to-heart reveal. She sat to my right but not nearly as close as usual. Though I tried to appear calm in her eyes, this scenario unnerved me.

With her left leg bent and up on the sofa, she sat listening to me. Under normal circumstances, the dimly lit patio under the stars and soft blue pool light to my left would be beautiful to share on a warm desert night. But at this moment, I wondered if the woman who had become my Stella Polaris would drag me down a black hole.

"My sister told me she overheard your conversation with some guy in your room while she was in the hallway," I began. She turned her head away and down and then turned toward me again, flustered with the corners of her mouth turned down.

"Michael, I don't know what you're talking about—there's nothing going on," she responded.

But I can tell when someone is not truthful—especially a woman with a kaleidoscope of smarmy, nonsensical, bereft excuses. When the truth is unbearable, the mind blanks out. But some ghost of the past event lingers long enough to raise its inescapable head.

"If you are seeing some other guy after all that we have been through, we are done," I continued.

"I didn't know how you had feelings for me," she driveled in hyperbole.

"I never expressed them in words—but my actions did," I reminded her. "Anyway, it's either him or me, or we are through," I emphasized one last time, calling her on the veracity of her statement.

"Then I will end it," she immediately assured me.

While her agreeing to drop the other guy felt satisfying for a moment, that response made it obvious that the heart-rendering betrayal was real, and perhaps her abandoning me would come next, rattling me to my core. When I began my day, I never envisioned it would end like this. Who knew what tomorrow portends? What I did not know then was that my best friend, sidekick, and wing-woman was the one who would inspire a book and perhaps help other fragile flowers, broken and torn petal by petal, like me.

"Even my best friend, the one I trusted completely, the one who shared my food, has turned against me" (Psalm 41:9, NLT).

CHAPTER 3: WORRYING

"I am with you and will watch over you wherever you go" (Genesis 28:15, NIV).

The day after Jenna's betrayal reveal in Arizona was full of as many fun things as possible to take our minds off the night before. There was no way an entertaining diversion couldn't be a quick fix to the previous night, which seemed like a fat chance. I went out of my way to restore a sense of normalcy by being an example of forgiveness to help make Jenna feel more comfortable since my sister was not so forgiving. The potential family tension left me worried. We all did our best to put the incident behind us as well as we could with lunch in Scottsdale Mall. We then took a ride at the nearby mini-Indy Car track, followed by laser tag and arcade games. With Jenna as my teammate and my little nephew's girlfriend, his wing-girl, we chased each other while laughing, partnering, and strategizing around a dark and scary maze.

Preoccupied with replacing worry with wit and brokenness with bonding, I was unaware that my laser gun was pointing at me the entire game, resulting in quite a laugh at the game's end. It may have been rather childish for adults, but sometimes innocent games can be the temporary ointment God uses to soothe aching hearts.

Our relationship consisted of numerous deeply thought-out and engaging heartfelt conversations from similar beliefs, values, and interests. But during the flight back from Arizona that night, things felt distant and awkward, even though we sat side by side. She was a little icy and withholding. Her aloof body language and preoccupation with doodling in her notebook left me sensing a coldness from her I had not felt before.

Here sat the one whose mysterious thoughts, hidden under her smooth white skin, was the refreshment I wanted to savor like a tall, thin glass of cool, refreshing milk with my favorite cookie. But sharing thoughts or dessert was not on her mind. When I dropped Jenna off at her sister's home near me after landing rather than her staying in my guestroom, it seemed as if it were all but over between us.

"Goodbye. Take care of yourself, Jenna," I said, holding her arms as I faced her outside the car, hoping she would grab my wrist and beg me not to leave or ask why I sounded so fatalistic—she said nothing.

Her face was a blank canvas, staring back at me with an apathetic gaze as if she was staring out a library window, pondering anything but the book in front of her. The book *The Secret* and the theme of *The Law of Attraction* popped into my head. She was a stone-cold walking example of the anti-Secret now. I stammered in my mind's voice a few clingy platitudes that hung limp in the ensuing eerie silence between us.

I felt held hostage by her apparent lack of response. At that moment, I felt invisible. It was like a final goodbye to me, for I sensed her heart was no longer with me. I was letting her go in my mind. She was moving to LA for a few months, so I resigned myself to the idea that it was over, at least for now. Why did I pick a lemon in the garden of love when only apples grow from the tree of knowing good and bad? There was no way to make sense of it all, knowing an ounce of her love could break my fall.

This goodbye did not go at all the way I hoped. I fantasized that she would throw one arm snug around my neck and pull my arm around her waist with the other in a slow-motion scene, like a soldier's fiancée clinging to his departing embrace. But nothing at all like that happened—*c'est la vie*. Not every breakup has to score a Tina Turner ending with you wiping your hands, "That's that," for I needed a little tenderness—thank you very much, Chris Brown. My eyes glossed over as I turned and walked away. Tears began to pour down my cheeks as I drove off. I spent the next few weeks of non-communication with Jenna navigating through a lot of worrying. To cope, I sought comfort in prayer, the Bible, and one Christian book after another. I listened to Christian podcasts, videos, and TV programs, for I had a lot to learn about dealing with anxiety and worry. It reminded me of a breakup shortly after college.

Long Ago Goodbye

I will never forget the last time I spoke to my first girlfriend after college. She handed me a blank college notebook with four hand-written sentences. "Michael, I know I can never replace your journal. I guess this is my way of saying that I am truly sorry for what happened. I hope that you can fill this new one with your future thoughts and emotions. I hope it will also become for you a book of happy memories—Crystal."

Those were the last words from a girl I had hoped to continue dating long after college. But it all ended when her previous boyfriend of several years came back into the picture. His relentless begging for another chance once he heard she and I had started dating weighed on her and led to their eventual reconciliation. I left my college journal with her dad that day, hoping she'd reconsider after reading a few pages. She never read one. Her dad disposed of it, not realizing what he had done.

He had no way of knowing it was a culmination of ninety-eight letters written over three years of college for my future wife. I held nothing against him—it was my mistake by leaving it. Her dad had prayed over our dinner with me as a guest, so I knew he was a good man. I attempted to rewrite what I called "Red Letters" again to my future wife, beginning with #99 for me and #1 for my future wife. My reasoning for calling them "Red Letters" was telling and noted in my journal: "As much as a business that falls in the red suffers great loss, so will be my life if I can never share these with you."

These letters included various songs and poems I had written for my future wife. I hoped that she would enjoy them one day. I wrote songs and played an electric guitar back then. But that all ended after I lost everything written in my journal. Now, I was facing a loss of enormous devastation with Jenna, one more important to me than the loss I had felt for my journal. While that journal meant the world to me, it was only preparation for finding the one to fill the void in my world.

Finances and Marriage

Many of the letters detailed a meticulous exactitude of various stock purchases and business transactions I had conducted. They were a part of my plan for securing a bright financial future for whomever I would one day wed. It included newspaper clippings of strategic business dealings managed in my early twenties. The letters could have become a book by themselves. "Many marriages would be happier if the husband tried as hard to keep his wife as he did to win her," I wrote. And here's another gem I penned back then: "A successful marriage requires falling in love many times with the same person." On another page, I quoted a few thoughts on sorrow years before ever imagining reading a book on the subject. "God teaches us lessons in the school of suffering that we can learn in no other classroom." There also was a quote that sounded like something intended for this book: "I've heard that when God denies us something, its purpose is always to give us something better." I may have been foreshadowing about my life back then without realizing it.

The journal also contained Bible verses and my thoughts on feeling "broken." I noted them decades before I ever thought of writing a book with that topic in mind in this excerpt from the rewriting: "I thought of Proverbs today and how an excellent wife is hard to find. But she is worth far more than jewels. This day is a reminder that even in laughter, the heart may ache in pain. It is a pain that squeezes your chest like the tightening and twisting of a taut rope. It squishes teardrops one by one. It is a part of my last conscious breath before sleep and the first thing to dread upon awakening." Those same feelings surfaced again when I thought of Jenna three decades later.

I've only shared one of the twenty remaining letters with Jenna and no one else. As my eyes tear up from words written long ago, I share one of the remaining letters I rewrote. It is Letter #116, never seen or read by anyone other than Jenna before now:

> My dear wife,
>
> If you only knew what things I have been reserving for you. I have saved myself only for you. The Lord has put this desire in my heart. It is hard to believe nowadays

that someone 24 would save himself for his wife. If it ever changes, she will have to be you before I even tell you. I can't imagine being with anyone but you. I have put away much for us. You will never have to work if you don't want to because I will someday make something out of my life. When I was 21, my broker told me that he had never met anyone my age who had saved up so much. I'm saving it for us.

How cute and innocent it all seems now as I look back. I only wish I could have remained as virtuous as I started way back then. Losing my most sacred possession of ninety-nine letters could have created a whirlwind of panic and worry, which could have followed me for the rest of my life. Would I be able to recreate any of what I wrote? How long would this process take? Would I mismanage future financial dealings after having lost records of well-planned transactions? Would it hurt my future wife that another woman almost read what I intended for her eyes only? And what about Jenna? Now that we were in a limbo state, what If we never got back together and she never got to read my remaining letters? I had a lot of potential worrying.

But God stepped in. His Spirit, His Word, and the words of others encouraged me: "Anxiety weighs down the heart, but a kind word cheers it up" (Proverbs 12:25, NIV). The comforting words of the Bible took away my worries and care, even though I was only able to rewrite twenty of the ninety-nine letters. God gave me this book to write in compensation, among so many other things over the years. Yet, I still worried.

The Medical Equation

Unfortunately, Jenna was not in perfect health, as much as I would have hoped for her sake. I was one of the few who knew of Jenna's medical conditions. She revealed that one of her issues caused her pain every day and would require a relatively routine and common surgery to remedy it. Given that it was an elective procedure, she had no insurance or the funds to cover the operation, pressing hard on the tenderest part of my prefrontal cortex. Knowing she could not afford the corrective breast augmentation that needed fixing, I fully intended to cover the $10,000-plus expense for her at an appropriate time in our relationship, even though she had no idea of my plan to do so.

Each time she brought the issue up, it took every ounce of restraint to hold back from blabbing my rescue remedy to her, but I wanted to go about my offer in an appropriate and respectful way, without coming off as trying to be manipulative. I remember my concern about her considering their reduction in size when it would come to the time for the doctor to fix the problem.

"I've never even touched them," I said, pouting, not as much to protest my preference in her current size, but to communicate that I was in this for the long haul, a permanent commitment that is, before her doing so.

"Don't worry. You will," Jenna assured me. Coming from someone as religious and conservative as Jenna, I took that assurance as confirmation that she saw me as a frontrunner for potential marriage.

I had already spent many hours massaging the knee she injured as a high school cheerleader. And I knew almost every inch of her body, having spent hundreds of hours airbrushing her numerous modeling photos for three years.

Jenna also had another genetic condition that required medication daily for life. None of this changed my feelings for her. It only intensified my desire to take care of her and make sure she knew I would never abandon her despite feeling she had done so with me. My sister would think I was crazy for wanting to assume such a responsibility, given her firsthand knowledge of the apparent betrayal, so I never mentioned it—not wanting her to think any more negatively about Jenna. She would only have unstintingly told me of all the reasons why I should move closer to family.

"I could introduce you to so many women that would love to meet a guy like you if you would only move to Arizona," she had said before. I can only imagine the matchmaking search it would have ignited had she known my intentions of paying off Jenna's medical bills before I had even proposed.

The medical issues only escalated my concern for Jenna and how it would all play out. It bogged my mind. No one would take care of her through travails and the ravages of time as I would, so why was she wasting her time? Life is short, and we were missing out on God's best for us by not sharing it as a couple while still young enough to do so. What was she thinking? This line of reasoning only added another element to the equation: I was knocking myself out with my fist, worrying over issues out of my hands and potentially no longer any of my business. So how did I deal with worrying?

Knowing Worry's Origin

Worrying is a battle of the mind that started the day my journal was gone. Years later, it reared its ugly head when Jenna and I said our goodbyes after our Arizona trip. Her voice had stopped, but the echo still lingered in my mind. Those concerned and pessimistic thoughts contributed to my broken view of the circumstances. The devil never ran out of fiery darts to throw at me while I was trying to move ahead.

I wondered if she was thinking about or missing me? Was she seeing this mystery guy, and if so, what was so special about him? I wondered if he was taller, more muscular, or younger than me. Were they intimate while I'd been saving myself all this time for marriage to her? If yes, how could she act with such insouciance? Would I forever blithely be compared to this loping shadow man should Jenna and I wed one day? She was not the kind of person who could morph into a trickster who would think it okay to multitask once committed to being faithful in front of friends, family, and an expensive cake. Would knowing any of these answers hurt even more than not knowing? I had set myself up for a rapid descent with this line of thinking, for sometimes, there are questions that no answers can ever explain.

Satan was content with me worrying and continuing to remain broken. As the original liar, he offered me the wrong way of thinking when I panicked about replacing my journal—and it continued with Jenna. When I listened to his lies instead of God's truth, my heart would race as I heard it beating through my plugged-up ears. My brow would get hot and moist, and my throat would tighten. My half-smile would only belie the anxiety I felt. A desire for nothing replaced my naturally healthy appetite. Even longtime favorites like Bazooka Joe and Wrigley's Spearmint gum lost their nostalgic comfort appeal.

I was listening to the devil's worst-case outlandish and concocted scenarios. But we do not have to listen to every lie or entertain every negative thought he puts in our heads. We can't choose every feeling or thought that comes into our minds from his attacks, but we can decide what to do with them. We can let them stay and fester or push them aside. It was up to me—just as it would be for you.

The devil didn't want me to have any hope of rising out of my situation, so I claimed that no weapon of his formed against me could prosper, according to Isaiah 54:17. "Greater is He who is in you than he who is in the world" (1 John 4:4 NASB). I decided to use God's Word to chase wrong thoughts away: "Whatever is true, whatever is honorable, whatever is right, whatever is pure, whatever is lovely, whatever is of good repute, if there is any excellence and if anything worthy of praise, dwell on these things" (Philippians 4:8, NASB). Our minds are mighty and resourceful, so it was crucial how I used mine. "For as he thinks within himself, so he is" (Proverbs 23:7, NASB).

This scripture alone let me know how important what I dwell on is because we will become what we think! So rather than worrying about what might happen, I thought trusting thoughts of the Lord. One way I did this was to look up Bible verses on trust and memorize them. I then repeated the verses aloud while riding my bike or walking or in my mind while swimming. Daydreaming about God's biblical promises rather than life's problems was a quick fix for worry.

Rick Warren taught this in *The Purpose Driven Life:* "When you think about a problem over and over in your mind, that is called worry. When you think about God's Word over and over, that is called meditation. If you know how to worry, you already know how to meditate." So that is what I did. I memorized over forty Bible verses related to what worried me and called them out through the trees, streets, and sidewalks as though they were even when they were not apparent in the present. I spoke words of truth and hope rather than consider the negative possibilities reserved for the hopeless. I muttered verse after verse with every stroke through the pool over and over in my mind, casting my anxiety on Him as my eyes glazed over the black lane line five feet below me. Like the water surrounding my body, I let the Word envelop my mind as if it were air to my lungs.

Choosing to Trust

There's a memory room inside my soul that needed my trust in our Savior to bypass worry and enter. In the middle of the room is an old, cracked silver safe shaped like a heart with a lock you need a key to open. Inside that safe are all my childhood hopes and dreams. I'd given Jenna the key to that safe, but she left and no longer had access to the room and, thus, its contents. So now, with the key-holder gone, I worried if I could trust God to forge a replacement or bring back its bearer.

The devil is behind our worrying, so I cast aside my worries in Jesus' name. Satan was the one putting negative thoughts in my mind. He put all kinds of anxious thoughts in my head about Jenna while she was out of sight. If she cared about me, did she miss me after taking off and leaving town for months? If she did end her relationship with this other guy, as she had said in Arizona, was there some other reason for her not contacting me from LA? I thought of her constantly. I counted the moments, hours, and days of separation. Pulling the garbage cans to the curb each Friday reminded me of another week's absence without any word from her. If she had thoughts of me, why were they silent ones? Yes, I had a lot of worrisome thoughts that came to mind that were none of my business anyway, and I needed to realize where they were coming from and toss them aside.

The devil tried to make my life miserable so I would blame God rather than trust Him. Satan sought to wear out my ability to make good and wise decisions by heaping worry and sadness onto my brokenness, so I sought strength in the healing only God can give. The devil wanted me to pay attention to the lies he put in my head. Jesus wanted me to dwell on the truth that He loves me and has a good plan for me, so I purposed to cast off negative thinking.

I believed God, who was aware of and saw my problems from His perspective, would take care of my situation if I trusted Him. That meant I had to give up my need to understand everything and depend on Him rather than myself. Tomorrow would have enough worries. I chose to trust God one day at a time: "Do not worry about tomorrow, for tomorrow will worry about itself. Each day has enough trouble of its own" (Matthew 6:34, NIV). Worrying was not in my vocabulary anymore, but not until I chose to trust in God.

I had no worries anymore when it came to my journal either. I may miss it now and then, but I no longer worry about it. I trust that God will remind me of any lost writings that were important enough to remember. I am also now more aware of and careful about my thoughts after reading *Battlefield of the Mind* by Joyce Meyer. Reading her book made me aware of the devil's tactics. I learned to replace fear with trust in the Lord by not listening to Satan's lies. You can choose to either worry or trust—you can't do both at the same time. I chose trusting God back then, and I continue now.

Reading the Word

I spend more hours in my Bible than on a journal now. It's helpful to journal your life, but I now invest my time in scripture more than expressing petty worries on paper. Time spent with God in His Word increased my trust in Him and decreased my worrying. My mind was like a seesaw. As my trust in God went up, worry, fear, and panic went down.

Increased time spent with God increased my faith and trust, but it also helped me discern what is right and what is not. Time and energy are precious and limited. I needed to use them with wisdom, focusing on what matters. Each moment spent with God was a good use of that time, for it displaced my worries, fears, and panic. As my walk with God grew closer through His Word, He showed me how to spend that time and energy wisely. "Your word is a lamp to my feet and a light to my path" (Psalm 119:105, NASB). The Bible also analogizes God's Word to a "sword of the Spirit" in Ephesians 6:17. A sword is something used in battle.

There was a battle for control of my mind and thoughts that I was unaware of. I needed a weapon to make a way through the darkness of fear and panic that comes with worrying. I wrested power from my Bible as akin to a lightsaber. It was my protection from the enemy, and it was a powerful light that cut through the darkness of despair. It became my weapon against the brokenness of worry.

Nothing to Fear

Not to spoil the ending for you, but everything is going to be okay. It is going to take time, which is why I have so much to share. It has been a long time since I lost that journal, and everything has worked out fine without it.

I was confident that Jenna would contact me again whenever she came out to visit her sister or see me, so I trusted God would work it all out. There was never anything to fear, for God is with fainthearted you and me. As God was with Joshua, He is with us: "I will never leave you nor forsake you" (Joshua 1:5, NIV). God further emphasized this point later in the book of Joshua: "Be strong and courageous. Do not be afraid; do not be discouraged, for the LORD your God will be with you wherever you go" (Joshua 1:9, NIV).

This promise is what God gave Joshua, and He gives us the same guarantee. Though it seemed hard to deal with my experience of abandonment and betrayal, instead of worry, "I sought the Lord, and he answered me; he delivered me from all my fears" (Psalm 34:4, NIV). God is never blind to our tears, never deaf to our prayers, and never silent to our pain. He hears and will deliver us from trouble.

I speak from experience. I did not get to spend Jenna's actual birthday with her that year. We went to church together, then shared lunch and a birthday dessert at our favorite restaurant after the fact. She also took the time to come back to town to drive with me and spend my birthday dining in Palo Alto. But we spent less time together that year than usual. Still, I fought worry, fear, and missing her by trusting God to work it all out.

God does not create a lock without its key, and He doesn't allow problems without a solution. If I wanted God to close and open doors, I had to relinquish my tenacious grip on the doorknob. God has a plan for our lives, and it is higher than what you or I can see right now. God is going to take care of us: "Out of my distress, I called to the Lord; the Lord answered me and set me free" (Psalm 118:5, ESV). We needn't be afraid of anything. Rather than trying to maintain control over my life, I had to abandon my will and relinquish it to God. This release of authority felt frightening and uncomfortable because I wanted to assist God. I had to resist that temptation.

Giving God Control

I needed to trust God with control of my situation. The safest place to be is behind God's metaphorical shield of protection while He fights our battles, so releasing control to Him was pivotal. According to Ephesians 3:20 (NIV), He "is able to do immeasurably more than you can ask or imagine." Unless the Lord builds the house, you labor in vain anyway (see Psalm 127:1). I couldn't trust God and live in fear and worry at the same time. I had to trust Him when I didn't know the answer. I had no control over my situation with Jenna or her actions while out of town, so my only choice was to give control to God.

At the very moment of uncertainty, I had to tell God that I trusted Him and believed He would fight my battles for me even when I didn't understand what He was doing. I told God, "I don't understand, but I trust you anyway and leave the problem in your hands." I had to trust Him when the answer was, "Wait." To do this, I had to release control and wait for Him to tell me when to proceed. I had to trust Him even when the answer was, "No." I did this by choosing to be obedient to Him, leaving the choice of yes or no up to Him. Not once does the Bible say, "Worry about it, stress over it, and figure it out." Over and over, it clearly says, "Trust God."

God's only way to show us He's in control is to put us in situations we can't control. I don't agree with people who say God will never put you in a situation you can't handle. He won't tempt you beyond what you can withstand (see 1 Corinthians 10:13), but He will sometimes allow circumstances beyond your control and ability to handle without Him because that is what happened to me. I know this is hard for those who prefer to believe otherwise. Jenna not contacting me was hard, so I understand. I feared that my breakthrough would never happen the way I preferred.

I rationalized that God would be okay with me helping Him a little bit. I told myself, "I better have a backup plan." I was in the fear and darkness of my circumstances, which were crippling my trust in God. I was in the limbo of not knowing. We do not know what the future holds, but God does! We are not alone—He is with us wherever we go (Genesis 28:15). I needed to relinquish my desire to run the show and let Him fight my battles instead. God has never failed me, been too late, or left me stranded.

God was already working on the things that worried me, so I did not need to give in to fear. Fear and anxiety robbed me of energy and sleep through slothful days and restless nights of dread. 1 Chronicles 22:13 (AMPC) warns against dread, fear's cousin: "Dread not and fear not; be not dismayed." They hinder prosperity. Dread is a precursor to fear, and fear never brings a blessing. It only leads to more worry. Instead of feeling concerned over the things that frightened me, I sought the Lord for courage. The only thing we should fear is the Lord, who obliterates every other fear.

My foolish pride got in God's way of releasing His power to assist me. I was only creating stress by not surrendering authority to God. Thinking about it now, it was the pressure going on inside me, not something going on around me, that caused me to worry. My internal motor was on full throttle, always running on overdrive and off course. So instead, I had to turn off the stress fueling my engine with anxiety over my circumstances by giving the keys and control of my problems to God and letting Him take care of my worries and concerns. I even took a moment to pause and listen to Carrie Underwood sing "Jesus, Take the Wheel." I knew worry would be right there when I came back and wouldn't go anywhere until I released it.

Realizing What Matters

I had to realize that, in time, it wouldn't matter. Losing my journal was no big deal when I realized my wife would have this to read one day instead. If it turns out that she is the one who inspired these writings, then all the better for her.

When we have a problem, God will do one of two things: He will either remove the problem, which is what we would prefer, or, if He doesn't remove it, He will give us the grace, strength, and ability to get through the problem. I have heard Joyce Meyer say that a thousand times, and now I use it in my daily prayers. Until I got to the point where I could accept either way, I continued to have a tough time with worry.

I had to rely on God to face my problems as they came rather than anticipating them. Now, when I start to feel afraid, I remember that the Lord is holding my hand: "For I am the LORD your God who takes hold of your right hand and says to you, Do not fear; I will help you" (Isaiah 41:13, NIV). I wish I had a magic wand that would make all my worries and fears go away. I wish I had a pill that would instantly cure all my problems. But if I had that pill, I'd probably abuse it and lose my need for God. One day I will look back and realize that I worried too much about things that didn't matter as much as I thought they did. Worry changes nothing. "Who of you by worrying can add a single hour to your life?" (Luke 12:25, NIV).

Worry Delays Healing

Worrying was only delaying my healing. Every time I complained about my past, I was pulling back the bandage from my wounded heart, exposing my pain. Do you think it was easy for me to share so many intricacies of my story with Jenna? No, for the most part, it was painful. Past reminders of hurt were the last thing I wanted to think about, but I knew opening up and revealing my truth was necessary.

Even past thoughts of good brought worry of whether I would ever regain such moments. For every memory of her, there was a melody playing in my mind, a photograph of every outfit she modeled and ever wore. But memory is hard to ensnare, even when you build a website with many pictures of it. Still, those photos remained as caged images locked in my brain, like my computer, even though I longed to escape from them.

I can still see her on that bright Sunday morning when I picked her up for church. Her slicked-back hair tucked under a broad-brim hat and snug-fitting, Jackie-O-style, cream-colored dress that draped to the knees leading to her designer heels all matched in unison. Her movie-star sunglasses and petite Chanel purse resonated with exquisite class sketched forever in my memory. She was the most stunning classic vision of elegance in all my years of shooting fashion models. Added to all this glamour and beauty were her wit and charm, which spelled the recipe for mesmerizing. Her style and taste were like my favorite flavors. She took my breath away and held it in the palm of her vanilla Gucci gloves. I wanted to go back in time and be the person who had no worries that the growing bond Jenna and I shared could ever unravel.

I had to stop focusing on my broken situation. If I continued to complain about what was wrong with my life, I was only going to get more of what was wrong: "Be careful how you think; your life is shaped by your thoughts" (Proverbs 4:23, GNT). Believe me. I've listened to others who never seemed to progress. This delayed their breakthrough. I didn't want to look at what I'd lost. I needed to focus on what remained in my life.

God has a good plan for every one of us. I only needed to walk into mine. I was looking for a more worthwhile purpose in life, so I set my mind and heart to seek and inquire from the Lord (1 Chronicles 22:19). As I did, I found a purpose for my life beyond my wildest dreams. Do you think I ever imagined writing a book like this? Never! I was a photographer going about my own business, but

God stepped in to do more than I could have imagined. But that required me to set aside all my fears and worries. They were only delaying my healing. I had to trust God more than myself and stop worrying by reminding myself, "When you go through deep waters, I will be with you" (Isaiah 43:2, NLT).

Contemplating Complicated Solutions

Concurring worry required me to stop trying to figure it out. Unnecessary worry only says, "I am smart enough to handle this on my own without God's help. I need to think of a way to solve my problem rather than leaving it in God's hands. By thinking about this long enough, I can come up with a brilliant plan to get out of this mess." No, I won't and didn't. It was hard because I usually had a backup plan, but God's way is best. I had to admit to God, "I am not smart enough to run my own life. I most likely caused my problem. I'm sure I did some dumb thing and don't even know what that is, so could you please help me, God? I need your wisdom. Please show me what to do." Worry was a conversation I was having with myself about things I couldn't change. Prayer is a conversation I can have with God about something He can change.

Worrying and stressing result in wrong choices. I once thought of a little worry as a sign of wisdom, but I have learned differently: "Do not be wise in your own eyes" (Proverbs 3:7, NIV). My complaining and fretting came from my determination to have my way. Thinking I could run my own life and do a decent job without God's direction was a mistake. Worrying demonstrated that I was thinking my circumstances were too difficult for God to handle, so I was going to help Him out a little bit. I didn't. It only made things worse. Leaving the plan up to God is why I let Jenna contact me that summer and fall if she wanted to see me rather than vice versa. Instead of coming up with a plan to bring her to me, I let God lead her. At best, my worrying said that my situation was too unimportant for God. This kind of thought is also a ridiculous notion, as proven by how much the Bible talks about how God loves us.

Trying to figure things out and coming up with my own insignificant plan because it matters little to God are wrong ways of thinking. Instead, I had to set my preconceptions aside. I confessed to God that I would try not to worry and let Him handle it. The cause of my worrying and fussing was planning and scheming without trusting God. Worrying doesn't change anything, but trusting God changes everything: "You do not realize now what I am doing, but someday you will" (John 13:7, NIV).

Trying Some Gratitude

Worry only makes it worse, so I replaced all my negative thinking with prayer and thanksgiving. I found that there were so many things to be grateful for if I would only take the time to focus on them. When I was afraid and worried, I was not thankful. And when I was not grateful, I was dishonoring God, who created me and made all things available to me.

The Lord plants peace in the garden of our hearts, but the weed of worry grows among the flowers. I had to let the Lord rid my garden of weeds by trusting Him through my brokenness. I started to thank Him through my depression and despair. Thanking Him amid my troubles is what let in the light that dried up the weeds of my worry. I now thank the Lord many times a day. It has become a key to conquering my worries.

There is a reason worrying precedes the next stage in my journey. That's because the next chapter covers suffering, which usually follows worry and most certainly did in my case. But before we do,

I'd like to close with a verse that gave me confidence when worry reared its menacing presence.

> "Do not fear, for I am with you; Do not anxiously look about you, for I am your God. I will strengthen you; surely I will help you, Surely I will uphold you with My righteous right hand" (Isaiah 41:10, NASB1995).

CHAPTER 4: SUFFERING

"Those who sow in tears shall reap with shouts of joy!" (Psalm 126:5, ESV).

*T*here was an ominous gloom of depression approaching, and I was unsure how to deal with it even though I knew a little about suffering and heartbreak. My ongoing familiarity with its shadow hovers over me like a dark, misty cloud of despair in Middle Earth. It clings as would soaking wet clothes stuck to my skin on a cold winter's day, dragging me down like a heavy backpack I wish I could leave behind. Its load feels crushing at times. It's the reason I'm wide awake writing this chapter at 3 a.m. Each time I wade deep enough into the thralls of memory's waters and reenter the recent past, sorrow drowns me as if cursed to face their coded biblical meaning, fascinating me. In a moment of desolation, a sagging sadness from nowhere waylays me through the cracks of my mind like a straight razor. Living through unrequited love with betrayal can be one of the closest things to hell on this side of eternity.

Experience has taught me a broken heart is unmistakable. When suffering, you feel, think, and care about nothing else, like an unquenchable thirst. You may be able to relate. When secret treachery came by way of the person I trusted most, my heart didn't just break—it shattered into a million pieces. Not only did my hopes for the future change, but I saw them stomped on, shaken, and kicked to the curb like dirt off used shoes. I was dying inside.

There's nothing quite like unabashed deception and betrayal unveiled through private social media postings. It lingers when the apathy and disrespect inflicted are by those you thought of as closest to you. It is dumbfounding when they are blind to the fact that you have access to their secret viewing. Losing all trust and respect for those you had cherished is devastating. It's compounded after having done something beneficial for the offender in the meantime. The insult added to the injury is blatant. No amount of money can cover this kind of debt, and no compensation is enough for this kind of treason. How do I know all this? Because I am living through it as I write. Fool me once, shame on you. Fool me twice, shame on me. I took umbrage with the treason and will no longer be the one played like fun house mirror tricks. Can you relate? I am done being a backup plan.

Birthday Shopping Spoil

It had been about a month since Jenna and I had spent any time together. Letting me know she would be in town for the weekend and wanted to spend it with me, we made plans. Earlier in the year, she had found a new frame online for the bed in my guest room, so it was only natural she would stay with me as usual. Dinner and a movie were on the menu but so was birthday shopping, for Jenna was intrinsically lovable, better than frosting on the cake of life. And without that frosting, my presumed glamorous life as a fashion photographer felt plain as a muffin. So I took her to Macy's, where she tried on a plethora of stylish outfits. She needed some new clothes, and I was happy to get them for her and see her wear them with me rather than only photograph her in them. The following day we went to church together, where she looked like a fashion model in the red, white, green, and black striped dress we had purchased the day before. She had to have a few photos, so I did a few professional shots outside that day.

The next day we were back at the mall, where we found a boutique with all the right fashions to go with her figure. She tried on various shirts, jeans, and dresses as I snapped cell phone pics to remember each one. When it came to decision time, she gave the usual little tilting of the head toward her favorites while I held my chin and pondered the choices. In the end, I got her every item she wanted, of course, along with a few extra suggestions I selected for her as well. Knowing her brand new fashions would be filling my guestroom closet, awaiting her next stay over, things were looking up. She left town with some of the items I purchased for her, with enough clothes hanging in the guest closet to keep me from pouting—an indication she would be back to wear them out with me.

Thanksgiving Invitation Reveal

A couple of weeks later, Jenna called and invited me to spend Thanksgiving at her sister's house, so, of course, I showed up bearing gifts. You may be able to guess what happened next. She made other plans with her parents out of town without informing me, but this was not the worst part. After sharing Thanksgiving with the prior potential sister-in-law who broke the news with decorum yet still treated me like family, the egregious truth came to light. I'll never forget the warm hugs goodbye, then getting into my car and checking social media before driving home. My no-show date was blithely introducing another guy to her parents for Thanksgiving—the guy she said she would end it with months ago in Arizona.

I sank into my leather seat like melted butter, observing the treacherous gaffe. I can still feel the instant change in my blood pressure and loss of breath from shock. It was as if the weight of the world were pressing in on me. I couldn't even react—transfixed. Stunned, I didn't know what I needed most in that moment—chicken noodle soup, a double dose of melatonin, or my pastor. When you first discover bad news, your initial reaction is like being told you're fired, or the test results are positive. The hall closet of my wondering mind was now an insufferable place of unclear safety protocol through uncharted territory.

After three years of devoting over a thousand hours to Jenna's hopes, dreams, and aspirations, I felt usurped and discarded like trash. I'd been unwittingly playing this game of love with one arm tied behind my back. Now our story was on hold. Baffled, I wondered how I must have rolled through every stop sign and ignored each red flag. When you lay dumped on the roadside with not even the garbage collector there to pick you up, you feel unwanted. You long for shade from the burning light of day and shelter from the cold chill of night, but there is no relief. A heaviness was weighing on my heart and a look of consternation on my face. When impropriety and despair replace a dream with no hope of fulfillment in sight, you feel broken.

You may be able to relate—we've all been there. The moment you think, "This is too much for me," something worse happens. And right when you realize, "I can't take anymore," something even more unbearable falls upon you.

As I learned more about what was going on with Jenna and this guy, it became a season of overwhelming heartbreaks and disappointments. One discouragement followed another then another, with each one escalating in intensity. It was a season of hell on earth that left me completely shattered on the inside, yet almost no one knew. My business was thriving and very profitable. My professional and personal life's outward appearance seemed successful to those who hired me, those I worked with, and my friends. But my Heavenly Father could see a deep, black hole I'd tumbled down, for I felt crushed inside, hiding my broken spirit from all but my sister—my staunch supporter. My most sacred hopes and dreams for the future seemed dashed or uncertain at best. All my accomplishments seemed meaningless, and the future looked bleak.

I needed spiritual surgery on my torn and tattered heart. My crushed spirit was something no human doctor could mend. I felt in utter disarray, broken in a way that only God could fix. I wanted to know His thoughts, and I needed clear direction and guidance from God. I needed a specific word from God to know what action He wanted me to take. I looked to the comforting words of the Bible—studying and memorizing more of it rather than only reading it. Proverbs 3:6 advises us to acknowledge God in all our ways, and He will direct our paths—so I did.

On the Warpath

A couple of weeks later, I recalled a Bible verse during my prayers before bed: "For God does speak—now one way, now another—though no one perceives it. In a dream, in a vision of the night, when deep sleep falls on people as they slumber in their beds" (Job 33:14–15, NIV). With that verse in mind, I did something unusual and asked God to reveal in my dreams what He wanted me to do.

"Lord, I do not know what to do about Jenna. The situation seems hopeless and lost. I need to do what you want me to do in this situation with her, not what the world is telling me, but what you want me to do."

I prayed this while kneeling beside my bed in the dark. I was too emotional and devastated to sense any clear direction from the Lord, even during my prayer. You might think asking God for guidance through a dream doesn't sound so unusual. Well, the only problem is that I pretty much never remember my dreams. That makes a difference now, doesn't it? But all things are possible with God: "What is impossible with man is possible with God" (Luke 18:27, NIV). I fell asleep that night clinging to my faith. At some point in the dark of night, I arose from bed with my eyes shut.

My mind was still caught up in a dream state as I somehow found myself sitting in my bathroom. In my dream, which was as clear as day and as bright as a night sky with all the stars visible, I was a cowboy. I had the cowboy hat, boots, outfit, and gun to boot! I was alone, surrounded, outnumbered, and outgunned by face-painted Indians on the warpath. They were circling me on their horses with seeming intent to fire their deadly arrows at any moment. There was no escape, no hope, and nowhere to hide. As I leaned my back against the one thing between me and certain death, I sank to the ground against a large rock. As I awoke from the dream, two words came out of my mouth while contemplating what to do in this dire circumstance.

The two words were "Do nothing." I spoke the two words aloud.

Now awake, I realized that the first two words out of my mouth answered my prayer request from the night before. It was an awe-inspiring moment that left me thanking the Lord for answering my prayer! I realized that the warriors represented everything that was coming against me. The rock served to represent God, sometimes referred to as the rock in the Bible. Little did I know it would be a while before God would tell me anything else to do. But after receiving a clear-as-day message from God about my actions, I spent the holidays tending to my grieving heart. I missed Jenna tremendously, but the only thing I knew to do was obey God's directive: Do nothing. So that's what I did.

Truth and revelation are sometimes stranger and more mysterious than fiction. They cut to the heart and soul. I have gone through a lot since that night of prayer, so I ask you to go on a truth-seeking journey with me. I invite you to consider the following truths I learned through my suffering process.

Life Is Short

When someone treats you like they don't care, as Jenna treated me, believe them. Nothing bamboozles a man like a sweet-talking mug and superfine body. Marina and the Diamonds described her well in the song "Primadonna." I am done being the one mesmerized by her beauty and acting skills. Charm is deceptive and beauty fleeting. A pretty face gets old, and a nice body will change. But a good woman will always be a good woman.

Life is short. Before you realize it, you are forty, fifty, or sixty and wondering, *Where did all that time go? It seems like only yesterday I was thirty!* So where will she be when I am the one gone like the roadrunner? In her fragility, will she suddenly realize the needs I have filled for so long? "For he knows how weak we are; he remembers we are only dust. Our days on earth are like grass; like wildflowers, we bloom and die. The wind blows, and we are gone—as though we had never been here" (Psalms 103:14–16, NLT). Life is shorter than we realize.

Pain Has Purpose

This scenario of truth revealed via social media is not something a simple prayer could take away. God's purpose is beyond our comprehension when we go through something hard. But I learned to take courage in knowing that God never allows pain without a purpose. "He's preparing you for what He's prepared for you," according to Pastor Christine Cane. No matter how much it hurt, I knew I would look back one day and realize it changed my life for the better. There was a purpose in my pain and a reason for the struggle. There are many sorts of broken hearts, and Jesus is good at healing them all. "…by His wounds, you have been healed" (1 Peter 2:24, NIV). Jesus didn't come for the ones who have it all together. He came to restore the broken, and that meant me. Jesus leaving the ninety-nine to find one seems crazy until that one is you.

I understand betrayal from the one I held most dear. It broke my heart because only she had access to it. My goodness, it affected me enough to write a memoir inspired by her. It was more painful than the grief of losing my most cherished pet, for she was the person comforting me through it. If your broken heart emanates from someone who did you wrong, someone gets it, and I don't mean me. I wrote *a book*, but He wrote *the* Book. Jesus understands very well what it is like when someone close to you betrays you. And in betrayal, He experienced disrespect. His betrayal was for thirty silver pieces, the lowest price you could put on someone at the time, showing they also undervalued Him. So, don't let it surprise you when someone undervalues you like it did me. The shock of being betrayed left me feeling undervalued, but we are worth more than gold in God's eyes. Our value is not in what others think of us or how they treat us. Our real value is in what God thinks of us, and He thinks we were worth dying for. "For God so loved the world, that He gave His only

Son, so that everyone who believes in Him will not perish, but have eternal life" (John 3:16, NASB).

God brought the greatest blessings from my worst of circumstances. He took my broken pieces and used them to make me into something better than before. When it makes no sense and I don't understand, I've learned to do one thing through suffering: trust God and do good (Psalm 37:3), which I will discuss later. I know God loves me so much that He let something happen to hurt me for a while only because it made me better in the long run. It made no sense at the time, but it made me a higher-quality person and a better empathizer.

God's Not Mad

I wanted to crawl inside a hole and bury my head, pretending this was not happening with Jenna, that it was all a dream. This kind of thinking was unnecessary, for it is God who engineers our circumstances, whatever they may be. I needed to face them while abiding in Him. Trials and tests are not necessarily evidence of God's displeasure or anger. They are tools He used to train and develop my faith while producing character.

God used my brokenness to build character in me I never knew I needed or for which I never volunteered. I learned that character doesn't develop through ease and quiet. It only comes through experiencing trial and suffering. It is an honor that the Lord has allowed me to suffer while doing good rather than for something I did wrong. God grew me up in spirit through suffering. It wasn't a punishment but a confirmation that He loves me. I accepted my pain and suffering without the need for God to explain. I get it. I already knew He had a better plan than mine, so I relinquished my dream of several years to Him. I have learned to let go and let God take control of my problems.

I hope you will be able to do the same through your suffering. God is fixing the broken pieces of my life. He is not mad at me. God is merely preparing me for everything for which I've been praying. Broken things can become blessed things if we let God do the mending. My failed attempts to grow this relationship into something that would lead to marriage led to idolizing it. God was working in a different way, though. He wanted to build character in me so He would be my idol rather than her.

My Hurt Pocket

My inner suffering left me emotionally scarred and damaged. It became a place to conceal my misery from others. Only when I decided to give my pain to God rather than let it fester did I begin the road to healing and recovery. And releasing that pain to God was a process, not a singular event. It was a long road of emotional surrendering my deepest desires and hidden secrets that allowed God to heal my wounded soul.

This suffering journey did not come with a quick fix God would deliver me with, but this was something He was taking me through instead. Exhausted and broken, I needed God to stitch the shattered pieces of my heart back together one by one, for they affected every ounce of my being. Often, all I could think about was how painful it felt inside. When I awoke, it was the first thing on my mind and the last thought before sleep. If not sufficiently preoccupied with some task, it came to mind. Even when busy, it sometimes overwhelmed me to the point of stopping me from what I was doing.

I felt like no one could understand, so I kept silent about the mental and emotional anguish going on in secret. I thought no one could relate. After all, I was usually surrounded by beautiful models to photograph. I dare not tell any of the jocks I knew at the gym who knew what I did for a living. They would not understand and only ask how one prized model could encompass so much of my thoughts with all the other eye candy at my disposal. As a growing Christian wanting to change his ways and perhaps his career, I did not think like that. They did not know that a dream had died inside of me, leaving me wondering how I could ever go on without her. It's a marvel no one could see that hidden behind the perceived life of any guy's dream was a boy only wanting his favored girl back. What others would have seen inside of me, if they could, was a broken vessel needing restoration. But those broken pieces were all God needed to mold me into the shape of a better person with a higher purpose and focus on Him. Jenna broke my heart, but God was there to wipe away my tears and help me overcome my worries, waiting, and wounds.

I had to trust that there is no wound so deep God can't heal and no pain so great He can't remove. This way of thinking required that I give God the deepest, darkest depths of my broken heart for the healing to begin. I needed to reset the Geiger counter of my desire from pointing to the precious metal of one woman's nature to seek the rock Who is higher than I. This decision put me on a path less traveled but one that would lead to freedom from brokenness because God wanted to patch up my "hurt pocket."

Could Be Worse

Ernest Hemingway won the 1954 Nobel Prize in literature. When asked if he could write a compelling story in six words, he responded, "For sale. Baby shoes. Never worn." Hemingway's story is compelling because it inspires us to fill in the blanks. Was there a tragic loss or death that led to the parents no longer needing the shoes? I have heard that no suffering is worse than the loss of a child. As I write this story, I recall back to only yesterday. A client who hired me for my photography and graphic services narrated her own sad story.

The memory of her son being shot in the head and killed only a few weeks prior was still in her daily thoughts. I was in shock as she explained the story in detail. There was little I could say to empathize with her. I knew I had met my match in the degree of brokenness, and her pain undoubtedly exceeded mine. I had lost a best friend and potential spouse when I saw that social media post—she had lost a child. I thank the Lord for sparing me from such grief. "Real suffering has a face and smell. It lasts in its most intense form no matter what you drape over it. And it knows your name," Mary Karr wrote in *The Liars Club*.

I informed her that I was writing a book on suffering and would address part of her story. That was okay with her because all she needed was a listening ear. It was one more confirmation that my story was necessary and inspired to help many people. If this book were already in print, I would have given her a copy and told her so. All I could do for the time being was to pray for her and be there. If losing a child is your plight, I have no words that qualify me to comfort you through your pain. But God qualifies the unqualified. For only God has the healing words that reach in and pull you out of life's most heart-wrenching torments. They touch the very framework of the soul. If your suffering is not the result of a death, recall Hemingway's six words and be grateful. God has spared you of worse pain.

No matter what, there is still hope for brokenness through the comforting words of the Bible. There is plenty of suffering in this world. No one said walking the Christian life would be easy. Ernest Hemingway also wrote, "We are all broken. It's how the light gets in."

God Sees Suffering

Everyone has heard the saying, "No pain, no gain." Suffering through brokenness in the Christian walk resembles that. God is there and aware. God heard my cries. His ear was close as He listened to my heart's desires amid my suffering: "You, LORD, you hear the desire of the afflicted; you encourage them, and you listen to their cry" (Psalm 10:17, NIV). Every time I prayed in secret, He heard. Every time I submitted to God's authority through mistreatment, He knew. Every time I quoted God's Word, even though my emotions were screaming, "This is unfair!" He would see. Every time I praised God through my brokenness, He saw and remembered. Every time I claimed the truth that I am special in God's eyes while feeling invisible, He agreed. Every time I felt insignificant or unimportant, I mattered to Him.

When I felt like the least likely or the last choice, He knew He made me in His image. Feeling alone, unwanted, and rejected, I remembered that nothing goes unseen by God. He is very aware of and observes all our suffering. He saw my tears and felt my pain: "You keep track of all my sorrows. You have collected all my tears in your bottle. You have recorded each one in your book" (Psalm 56:8, NLT). That is so awesome! When it hurt so bad that I couldn't speak, God saw all my tears. He is aware of our suffering.

These are some of the verses that got me through every day of my suffering. I memorized them so I could quote them back to God for daily hope. It was such a comfort to know that God was aware of all my suffering and wanted to heal me everywhere I hurt. That included my emotional and physical health.

If you are grieving like I was, He wants to award you a crown of beauty instead of ashes with joy instead of mourning. And He wants to clothe you in a garment of praise instead of a spirit of despair (see

Isaiah 61:3). He wants to give you favor even though you do not deserve it. Instead of your former shame, He wants to restore you with double compensation (see Isaiah 61:7). And for your suffering, He wants to give you everlasting joy.

God's Got Us

The word recompense means repayment. So, when I read Isaiah 61:7, which says that God will repay me for my dishonor and shame, it means He will make up for all my hurts. It was a relief to learn that God would provide me with justice one day. "'VENGEANCE IS MINE, I WILL REPAY,' says the Lord" (Romans 12:19, NASB). If someone has hurt you, as someone broke me, it is natural to want your inflictor of pain to suffer. I did not want my unwitting inflictor to suffer. I loved her. Instead, I had to forgive. Not everyone treats us the way we would prefer. But God has our backs, and He will make it up to us if we trust Him to do so. We only need to put our faith in Him, inviting Jesus into every area of our lives so that He can make us whole.

Too Self-Focused

I was focusing on myself too much. God will undoubtedly get our attention at the right time if we desire to be close to Him. What He does for one, He does for the other: "For God does not show favoritism" (Romans 2:11, NIV). His promises are not for someone else—they are for us all. I knew God loved me and had good intentions, so I believed that He had an excellent plan that was better than mine.

But I had to prepare myself for some schooling in the suffering department. It was necessary to smooth out my rough edges to grow in the Lord and be the best version of myself. God kneaded me into broken bread and poured out wine to please Him and nourish the souls of others. It was something I learned the hard way.

When it came right down to it, I was too self-centered. Selfishness indeed was the disease of "me," for you cannot be selfish and happy. Even if I had gotten everything I wanted, it wouldn't have made me happy. Happiness comes from giving yourself away for the sake of others rather than being selfish. I was unhappy because I spent all my time thinking about my problems.

I asked God, "If you are all-powerful, why are you not removing my pain?" But I admit that if He had done that, I wouldn't have learned much. One of God's purposes in allowing my suffering was so that I would understand the needs of others better. To gain this kind of understanding required empathy. It called for some experience with similar problems and hurts that others face. This experience is what I needed to learn to share these words. By experiencing some of what others go through, I could better empathize with them. Suffering removed a great deal of my selfishness. Sometimes, we can only find who we ought to be by going through a few sorrows of our own. Some people don't care about others, or they may even judge them. But when you go through rough times yourself, compassion increases. It doesn't have to match what they are going through. It is amazing how caring and compassionate you become if you experience a few problems of your own. I now understand why I have experienced some recent sorrow-filled revelations. In the past twenty-four hours, I have borne the brunt of disrespect and rude treatment by eight different people.

The self-centeredness came in the form of selfishness and impoliteness in return for my kindness. A friend, a co-worker, a customer, a client, and a total stranger all demonstrated the same rude behavior. It was dumbfounding at first, coming out of nowhere in a short amount of time. Then it hit me—God must have been schooling me with something He wanted me to add to my story. Case in point: I needed a little refresher in empathy, selflessness, and not judging others. I needed to feel how innocent people who are not treated kindly or with respect can feel. I needed to strive to treat others as I would want them to treat me in return.

Suffering Is Temporary

God used the wise counsel of others to minister to me during my brokenness, but God did not speak only through my ears. He primarily communicated with me through my circumstances. God may have allowed me to experience disappointment, grief, and heartache for a season, but my brokenness was only for a time to teach me that only He and His Word are what satisfy and restore. His Word is unshakable and especially vital to guide us through broken times. Psalm 126:5 (MEV) is one of many passages I turn to in prayer during such times: "Those who sow in tears shall reap in joy."

Another verse that brings comfort in suffering is 2 Kings 20:5 (NIV), which says, "I have heard your prayer and seen your tears; I will heal you." I paraphrased those words with thankfulness back to the Lord for comfort and strength when Aslan died and many more times when Jenna left me. I thanked Jesus that He replaces tears with joy and that He is the healer of the brokenhearted. I thanked Him that my trials would one day end in comfort. I didn't look at my circumstances thinking they would never change. I just needed to imagine myself succeeding on the inside even before it showed up on the outside.

Suffering Has Purpose

Through my pain, I experienced three typical stages on the road of suffering. Either I was currently in a trial, coming out of a one, or going into one. It reminded me of driving up and down the streets of San Francisco. So, I asked myself, *How can I make the most out of my time of suffering, not wasting the sorrows?*

Whatever we go through, we won't get to relive this moment again. So, no matter how bad it seemed, I considered it an opportunity to learn something about myself and a way to grow closer to God while learning through my pain. It wasn't my preference, but I had to take advantage of this moment anyway. I may never again experience something like what I was going through again. Aside from the one time I overreacted and raised my voice at Jenna in reaction to something she did not realize had hurt my feelings, I never treated anyone as well as I had treated Jenna and yet was cast aside. There was too much to learn from this not to take this moment to learn from my pain. I didn't want to waste this unique opportunity to gain valuable lessons and grow closer to the Lord. If this broken situation had not occurred, I would have missed out on this course in the schooling of life. When God wants you to grow, He makes you uncomfortable. All suffering seems unpleasant and undesirable while experiencing it, but I learned to greet it by anticipating the valuable wisdom I would acquire.

No one wants the heartache that comes with brokenness, but I concluded that I would not exchange what I learned about worship, worry, and waiting for a speedy end to my problems. What I learned from the experience about trust in God, prayer, giving, and doing good for others brought me closer to God and equipped me to comfort others who suffer. Early on, I was not ready to embrace the pain, recoiling back from the suffering. But I embraced it while it was fresh enough to help others and myself in the process. You see, sometimes God will allow us to go through pain in life for the primary purpose of helping someone else. Going through the fires of my sorrow has allowed God to use my suffering to nourish others.

All suffering has meaning in God's kingdom. That was a comforting thought when hopelessness seemed like my only familiar friend. My pain and problems were an opportunity to trust God. Braving my circumstances and even thanking God for them is one of the highest forms of praise. This kind of thanksgiving rings bells of attention in heaven. I could not run from my pain or hide from my problems. I had to trust that God had a plan. Accepting adversity in the Lord's name caused hope and peace to emerge from the ashes of my heartache. Giving praise and thankfulness to the Lord amid my grief allowed Him to fill my heart with joy, knowing He had a purpose.

Suffering Develops Character

My suffering produced endurance. Endurance then produced character, and character led to hope. I soaked in this schooling, listening over and over to the wise preaching of Pastor Eric Mason. While experiencing the same things he spoke of in my own life, I clung to his words of hope. I never actually took the thought of rejoicing during my sufferings seriously. Even though I had read it in the Bible before, until Pastor Mason pointed it out to me, it didn't click.

"God utilizes suffering as a means to grow us spiritually in the midst of our difficulties," he would say. It's like my working out was conditioning to perform at my best physically. "Many times, in trials, the brokenness of suffering can send you into a place where hope is lost," he would add. In that case, it is okay to tell God, "I don't know what the heck is going on, but I trust you." Even Job said in Job 13:15, "Though he slay me, yet I will trust him." I needed to trust that God was working out everything for my good and had my best interest in mind. Even though my suffering was painful, I eventually embraced it. The character it produced enabled me to see beyond my current circumstances, which gave me hope of a preferred future. "The righteous person may have many troubles, but the Lord delivers him from them all" (Psalm 34:19, NIV).

God Gives Hope

My suffering looked unfair and so hard at its onset. My problem seemed too unique and hopeless to fix. I felt that I was getting nowhere at the beginning. I later learned this reaction was typical and that I may even have to "go through" more before I "get through" it all. When I thought I had finally gone through enough, I had to go through even more. It felt like it was more than I could bear. I asked God again and again, "Why?" But in the end, as I pressed on, I eventually said, "Now I get it!" Even while experiencing pain, I clung to hope for a breakthrough, and God gave me little mini-deliverances of hope along the way.

These little timeouts from my pain would show up in different ways. It appeared in the form of good news through a text from Jenna, an encouraging Bible verse, and an appearance of resolution to the problem. An uplifting sermon, a word of wisdom, a dream from God, or a phone call would give me a timely, uplifting boost. In other words, God provided me with some relief amid my suffering. The glimmer of hope was encouraging, but I learned they were only small deliverances before full deliverance from my misery. I have had times that were trial-free, but this was a time when I was "baptized" in the fire of trials. Through it all, God gave me hope.

Suffering Demands Attention

Suffering was an isolating thing that got my attention, even in a crowd of people. I felt alone with God via heartbreak and the disappointment over my broken relationship with Jenna. At first, my crushed and humbled heart left me speechless, unable to utter a question to God. I believed God could heal me and found that I could relate to Oswald Chambers after reading *My Utmost for His Highest:* "As you journey with God, He comforts your soul." My sorrows and problems were confusing. I thought I understood other people's struggles; then God disclosed similar shortcomings in my own life.

I had vast areas of selfishness and ignorance that the Holy Spirit revealed to me when I sought Jesus. It took suffering to get me to that point on my knees. It reminded me of a typical hospital scene on a daytime soap opera. The only time they call on God is in desperation. Usually, they need a miracle healing or relief from inescapable pain and suffering. I learned that this way of healing is not how God operates. He wanted my attention through the good and the bad, as I learned having read Psalm 50:15, James 5:13, and 1 Thessalonians 5:17.

Suffering Seems Senseless

Sometimes, there is no explanation for suffering in this lifetime. It doesn't always make sense. I recall the most popular girl in my school in the seventh grade. I can picture myself back in junior high in my mind's eye. Her beauty resembled that of a young woman. Being a year older than I was, she did not look or act like a typical eighth grader. Her popularity was the only thing that stood out more than her long blonde hair and five-foot-eight-inch frame. Her face was that of an angel. A crowd of onlookers always surrounded her, and she was never alone as she walked through campus. She would undoubtedly grow up to be the high school prom queen and then a model or actress someday, so I imagined.

One day, I came to school to learn with shock the story that consumed the whole school with grief. The night prior, only one block from my house, this girl was tragically struck by a car and dragged to her gruesome death. The entire school was in a stupor of mourning. I could only imagine what her parents were going through. Twelve-year-old me felt sorry for them.

These are the times when there are no words of explanation for suffering. Only God knows the answer, and He's not telling. Sometimes, this life seems full of sorrow and is much too short. And yet God knows the number of our days before they happen, as David wrote in Psalms: "…in Your book were all written the days that were ordained for me, when as yet there was not one of them" (Psalm 139:16, NASB). I have experienced the death of nine blood relatives and nine pets in my short lifetime, so while it was sad, it is comforting to know that none of it was a surprise to God.

I have also experienced senseless suffering that did not involve death. I have a sister I grew up with who left home when she turned eighteen, right before my high school freshman year. I've only seen her twice since. I also have two sisters I've never met and a stepsister I only spent a few days getting to know and never saw again. And recently found out that I may have had an older brother who passed away before we ever met. The picture of him sent to me looked like me at thirty but with curly hair and a beard. He also looked like my dad. But for you, all that pales in comparison to whatever pain you are going through right now. And that is okay. Perhaps your suffering led you to this book to guide you directly to the helper and healer of all. I know nothing seems more ever-present and real to you than your own story of brokenness. It fills your mind at this moment. I get it. I realized that in this life, we might never understand completely, and that's okay, too. One day, in this life or the one to come, we will.

Through my suffering, I asked God, "Why is this happening?" and "When will this or that happen?" God did not take me aside and explain everything to me. It would have been nice, but that's not how He worked. Instead, He explained certain things to me as I could understand them. I have spent thousands of hours listening to Joyce Meyer online and on TV. One of the phrases I have heard her say, I have experienced myself: "We live life forward but understand it backward." There is so much truth in those words of wisdom. Jesus Himself confirmed that phrase when in John 13:7 (NIV). He said, "You do not realize now what I am doing, but later you will understand." Joyce is famous for her robot impersonation while using the phrase, "What about me?" repeatedly. It's a humorous example of my own foolish thinking and how I often question God during times of uncertainty and suffering.

What's not so funny is that my attitude needed some adjusting. I was mad at God for allowing me to suffer so much. My brokenness was not my problem; my attitude toward my brokenness was the problem, and Proverbs 3:11–12 (NIV) clarifies why God may allow disappointment: "My son, do not despise the LORD's discipline and do not resent his rebuke, because the LORD disciplines those he loves, as a father the son he delights in." The next time I find myself asking God, "Why?" or "When?" I'll know His answer is, "Because I love you."

God's the Restorer

Though I knew Jesus loved me, I thought my suffering was almost too overwhelming to handle. Whether in books I read or videos I watched, the world tried to tell me that psychology was the answer to my pain. But the truth is more straightforward than that. God gave me things I couldn't handle or control so that I would rely on Him to manage them for me. I thought my situation was so unique that no one could understand. I couldn't watch any drama on TV. For months, I couldn't listen to music without tearing up. The answer was not in a pill, potion, or psych session. God restores the broken things in our lives (see Joel 2:25). There is nothing too broken for God to repair.

One day everything that broke me God will use to restore me. I knew God would put me back together and make me stronger right in front of the one who broke me. I needed to learn that sometimes God will take away someone you think you need so that you will depend on Him and not a person.

Suffering Brings Good

Suffering is a fact of life. It did not care if I was rich or poor, black or white, male or female, young or old. I just had to hold on and not give up or lose hope. Nothing in this world is permanent, not even our problems. "The righteous person may have many troubles, but the Lord delivers him from them all" (Psalm 34:19, NIV). I had to trust in the Lord for a brighter future. It does not cost anything to hope for the best. My most potent message came out of my deepest hurt. Birthed out of the most severe heartaches are some of the greatest blessings. Good can come from suffering.

What is painful for today will be profitable for tomorrow. The pain I felt can't compare to the coming joy (see Romans 8:18). And just because I didn't see a way doesn't mean that God didn't have a way to solve my problem. God will make a way when there seems to be no way (see Isaiah 43:16, 19). Life's most considerable difficulties often happen right before life's most significant breakthroughs. In time, my miserable life will become a thing of the past, and my suffering will soon end. Time does not heal. God heals in time.

Engrained in my mind is the rush of excitement that sat me upright in bed the morning Jenna called and invited me to join her and her family for the holiday. My patience paid off. I wondered how she would introduce me to family members I had not met yet. I imagined that a Christmas invitation and New Year's Eve as a couple would be a shoo-in after this family inclusion. But seeing her mountaintop post with my rival at sunset, followed by his inclusion in her family photo, left me blindsided with a crippling blow of sudden heart palpitations. The apparent end of my relationship with Jenna felt like the end of the world I had planned and envisioned. But God turned the light on when I was in utter darkness and led me to a discovery. Some of my most significant blessings are those that come wrapped in painful and agonizing disappointment.

There was a purpose to my pain, and it was not because God was mad at me. God gave me things I couldn't handle so that I would rely on Him to manage them for me. He saw my tears and felt my pain. My pain was temporary and my heartache a learning experience, so I didn't waste my sorrows. It didn't make sense, but it developed my character. God made me like broken bread and poured out wine to please Him and comfort others. So much good came from my suffering. That good result was of utmost importance since my traveling companion covered in the next chapter was a troubling type of pain—loneliness.

"He heals the brokenhearted and binds up their wounds" (Psalm 147:3, NIV).

CHAPTER 5: HOLIDAY

"Even in laughter the heart may ache" (Proverbs 14:13, NIV).

Sitting at the terminal gate as I waited to board my flight was telling this holiday season. From my perception, it was clear this Christmas in particular that so many like me were hurting inside. I may not have seen the lingering aftereffects my broken heart still copes with on the sullen faces of others, but I could see pain. If the one you love betrays you, you gain experience in hiding sorrow. When that initial hint of indiscretion comes to light in the family's home of her first introduction, it screams inappropriate at best. If the revelation takes place during your last visit, it isolates you, magnifying loneliness at the next. When the suspected traitor is your best friend, you have fewer trusted places to go where you can conceal suffering. Of course, she said she would end it once I confronted her, but we all know that rarely happens, and it would be six months before I would know for sure. That Thanksgiving confirmation of Jenna's betrayal via social media left me with few places to go for solace.

You can't run to your family for comfort when they already know, having exposed the initial unexpected news. You can only hide among strangers in such revealing circumstances—a place where you can get lost in a sea of people. The airport is one of those places. I know what it is like to hide grief and crumbling heartache behind a smile, so I watch and learn from observing others. You see it on the fake smiles that permeate and last long enough until the head turns aside, and the Bible concurs: "A glad heart makes a happy face; a broken heart crushes the spirit" (Proverbs 15:13, NLT).

While contemplating my unexpected singleness, I observed the bored-looking couple to my left. The disgruntled couple to the right, who looked mad at each other without apparent provocation, reminded me of something I had read in one of Dr. James Dobson's books. It was so enlightening that I never forgot it. It read, "A bad marriage is worse than the most lonely instance of singleness." Being single, I have always been a little embarrassed to admit just how many books I have read on marriage. I only wanted to be ready with the wisdom and caution needed not to be a statistic one day. The funny thing is, I never got around to practicing what I learned except for advising others.

As a photographer, I photographed a lot of weddings early in my career. It provided opportunities for hundreds of conversations with women about marriage at receptions. As someone who has, in thirty years, interviewed over 10,000 women who wanted to model, I listened to many ventilate the horrors and blessings of dating and marriage from the female perspective. I learned of the duly portentous, Cropsey creep, shoddy-mannered, bombastic-speaking mountebank, liar, pugnacious, cheater, and similar ilk. And yet, here I am, a well-informed bachelor still waiting for the boarding call to marriage and Christmas in Arizona. I prefer not to spend another holiday single or traveling on my own with only my cat waiting at home.

In life, it's not where you go. It's who travels with you that matters, and a July–August 2019 survey seems to concur. The study of 10,000 Americans by Cigna discovered that three out of five people admit they are lonely. I cope with these facts by reminding myself to stay focused on what matters. And what matters most is that God is in control and will work it all out in His timing, which is better than mine. He will deliver the right person when the time is right while protecting me from the wrong one until then. In the meantime, I'll continue my vicarious observation of other travelers.

People-watching is a habit of mine, and the airport during a holiday is the perfect place for it. There are throngs of people everywhere waiting to board their plane. Communication was my minor in college, so I practice it now in prose and eloquence when appropriate. One of the things I learned was how to notice the insincerity of replete facial expressions. It was an unexpected bonus acquired in a nonverbal communication course. That course ignited my photography career and led to me working with thousands of women. No one else in my industry has interviewed and worked with so many female models and then entered the battlefield of Christian writing. That unique life education plus extensive biblical research and broken-heart experience give me unusual insight.

Inching closer to my plane's entrance in this slow-moving line, I pondered a different kind of takeoff. It is unheard of to be planning a departure from the perceived glamorous life of every guy's dream to instead inspire the broken with God's Word. But that early retirement from a long, rewarding career for another, more altruistic calling is what I was contemplating. As these thoughts raced through my mind, the gorgeous flight attendant ahead of me smiled at me with one raised eyebrow. I had remained faithful to my wing-woman in all possible ways, whether she knew it or not. I continued to look out for her best interests even after deceit.

Take a journey with me this day as I traverse the road of loneliness on the wings of contentment. I hope the way less traveled will be as interesting to you as it was helpful to me.

There's No Rush

Working with many women over the years, I have heard every beleaguered and painful story imaginable about marriage and divorce. They far outnumbered those in the many books I have read on the subject. As I boarded my cramped Phoenix-bound plane in seemingly slow motion, I coupled these insights with my current thoughts. If you are single by default or married and looking for an escape, you may feel as alone as I did on this holiday. Still, I'm resolute in choosing my spouse carefully. One thing is clear to me: being single and feeling lonely is better than feeling alone in an unhappy marriage.

It is better that I stay single until someone complements my life in a way that makes it better. If not, it isn't worth it. "An excellent wife is the crown of her husband" (Proverbs 12:4, NASB). I want that, but I'm not in a hurry. I've met hundreds of separated and single mothers who were just as lonely when they had a significant other.

Letting God Choose

As my eyes drifted from my window seat view, I noticed the person next to me blithely swiping away on what looked like a dating app. The last thing I wanted to think about was the possibility of the girl who meant so much to me doing likewise. We had so much meaningful and unfinished history between us, which was still ongoing, but betrayal makes you imagine the worst in everything. It is hard to let go when you don't have a sense of peace in that choice. I knew God brought Jenna into my life with a purpose, and I did not want to doubt Him. I wanted to trust that He would work all things out for my good with her or bring me someone even better. I did not need a reminder of the world's alternative.

I then began thinking of a friend who thinks she is too busy to meet the right guy, so she dates online only to complain it never works. Even though she lives in a densely populated city, she searches far and wide like one might attempt to slake a doozie of thirst in the Arizona desert. I often remind her that God knows where she lives. She doesn't have to spend her free time tracking down a mate. God knows where to find her when the time is right. Nowhere in the Bible are we told to spend our time and energy looking for a mate. Instead, God wants me as a single person to seek Him first: "Seek ye first the kingdom of God, and his righteousness; and all these things shall be added unto you" (Matthew 6:33, KJV). I do not need to be on a mission to find or convince "the one." I need to connect with the one who knows where "the one" is. I may be single and feeling lonely, unfulfilled, and sometimes tempted, but I have come to realize something.

There are gobs of lonely, unfulfilled, and tempted married people out there. I have met a myriad of them myself over the years. In America, at least half of them want to escape their marriage enough that they divorce. That is a sad reality for the single-but-hoping. I would not board a plane if 50 percent of the flights did not have safe landings. I trust God's guidance in the picking and choosing. He has always been 100 percent right. Proper attention to God's leading and timing makes the wait easier and the choice wiser for me.

Marriage No Cure

As my plane landed, I missed the companionship of the woman who had stolen and then broken my heart, but don't get me wrong. I know that marrying her or anyone else will not cure my loneliness. That is unrealistic and too preternatural a weight to place on any marriage.

Exiting the plane and viewing the frenzy of families meeting and greeting, I reflected on the facts: Half of the couples that marry in the U.S. get a divorce, which means half the couples in this airport are doomed to a similar fate. And for those who stay together, many are unhappy. I see it in their posture and interaction with each other. It's on their callous, tepid facial expressions in a setting that should aptly inspire some enthusiasm or glee.

If you are single like me and fighting off that lonely feeling, the Bible points out that it could always be worse. "Better is a dry morsel and quietness with it than a house full of feasting with strife," as it says in Proverbs 17:1 (NASB). "Enjoy your dry morsel in solitude," I tell myself. It is better than a marriage and family full of nonstop bickering. It is also better than a broken relationship. Yet it seems that all I can think of at this moment of watching others greeting each other at the airport is my pathetic singleness.

When you love someone who suddenly seems to hardly notice your coming or going, it's worse than not getting along. I call it passive control, and I experienced some of this myself. Most of the time, Jenna would greet me with an endearing hug that would almost knock me over. Other times, she might pass me by like I was not there, leaving me feeling invisible. Yet even neglect could not wither away my feelings for her. This dominance factor is why many people I have met stay in abusive relationships. At least they're paying some attention to you. When this controlling or abusive type of relationship ends, I tell them to take courage. I've learned that heartbreak is a blessing from God. It's His way of letting me realize that He saved me from the wrong one.

Romantic heartbreak is unmistakable. There is nothing quite like it. You think of, feel, and care about nothing else. Sleep seems to be the only escape from painful, permeating thoughts, tears, and dreary expectations for each day. I knew from John 10:10 that this path was not God's way. Emotional pain lowered my ability to reason, problem-solve, and function. Concentrating on work, exercise, or eating a scrumptious meal that now appeared bland was difficult.

Exiting my destination arrival gate, I was deep in thought at this point. It was here that I reminded myself of Proverbs 18:22 (BSB): "He who finds a wife finds a good thing and obtains favor from the Lord." I want the kind of added favor that comes with marriage, which has escaped me throughout my entire life of singleness. I know marriage does not cure loneliness, but I want a godly wife, glimpses of which I saw in Jenna. I know what I want, or at least have a good idea. That may sound familiar. If it does, let me encourage you with the words I have said to myself: if only I would pursue God as much as I think of someone who doesn't want me, my life would be so good. As a suitor, if only my sweetheart and I sought God with the intensity I desired her, that would make for an ideal marriage. I liken it to a triangle with God at the top, the husband and wife at the other two corners surging up.

My desire for Jenna was so strong that I needed to be careful. I might end up married one day, still lonely and unhappy with the result. In his classic book, *Think and Grow Rich,* Napoleon Hill stresses something relevant. He teaches that knowing what you want and having a single "burning desire" and determination is key. The Bible says something similar when it comes to knowing God: "You will seek me and find me when you search for me with all your heart" (Jeremiah 29:13, NIV). Since a strong desire is so powerful, I best use it to seek God rather than a spouse, for He comforts in ways a mate cannot.

I've met many women in broken marriages. They wanted to rid themselves of their spouse or had a spouse who felt that way about them. Their problems were worse than mine and millions of other "single but looking" people out there. Wanting a mate is better than wanting a divorce or a different mate. It seems we are all a little broken. But the last time I checked, broken crayons still color the same. If you have gone through a divorce, I realize your pain is tremendous and may yet remain. I have listened to many women from broken relationships over the years. So many of them were single moms that I lost count years ago.

I've read the books of those respected and more knowledgeable than me on dating and marriage. I've researched every possible Bible verse on the subjects I could find, and I've listened to countless Christian sermons. I've also experienced God removing every girlfriend and potential girlfriend from my life only to thank Him for doing so later. All this has led me to some conclusions. If God can remove what I never expected to lose, He can replace it with what I never imagined having. The world offered me its version of a toolkit on how to handle and cope with a broken heart, but God knows what's best and has a better plan for me. "'I know the plans I have for you' declares the Lord, 'plans to prosper and not harm you; plans to give you hope and a future'" (Jeremiah 29:11, NIV). When couples love God first, they love each other better.

God Loves Me

I know Jenna will always love me and compare how well I treated her to how every other guy she meets treats her. I'm sure she will feel lonely at times pondering that too. I also know God has a good plan for me and her, whether she realizes it or not. He has our best interests at heart. I don't have to spend another day, let alone a holiday, in sadness. Instead, I have total peace knowing God loves me.

These serendipitous statements are beautiful, yet I was fighting them. If God loved me so much, why was I so broken and lonely in this crowd of travelers? But deep down inside, I knew that God loved me and had an excellent, purposeful plan in all my suffering. I pondered this assurance while still in the Phoenix terminal, walking toward the baggage claim. I know God will work every aspect of my desire for marriage for the best if I give it over to Him. Opening my Bible reminded me of this. "Delight yourself in the LORD; And He will give you the desires of your heart" (Psalm 37:4, NASB).

Jesus Understands Feelings

"Jesus wept," found in John 11:35 (NIV), is the shortest verse in the Bible, but even its simplicity tells me that He knew emotional pain. He knew sorrow: "My soul is overwhelmed with sorrow to the point of death" (Matthew 26:38, NIV), and "Jesus often withdrew to lonely places and prayed" (Luke 5:16, NIV). These tell me that He felt sorrow, like many who are lonely, so I know He understands when I feel lonely. Jesus undoubtedly felt very alone when Judas betrayed, and Peter denied knowing Him. Jesus understands loneliness and abandonment from those He loved and who said they loved Him.

Walking to the terminal exit, I noticed a despondent-looking fellow sitting near a garbage can. Loneliness is not solitude; even Jesus often withdrew from crowds to be alone. Loneliness is not isolation either. I've felt lonely in a group, and this airport, replete with passengers crowding and scattering in all directions, increased that emotion. One happy-go-lucky couple looking acid-reflux-inducingly in love left me feeling vexed being solo when I should have been happy for them. It was a pitiful sense of feeling unwanted, unneeded, and unnecessary.

I've read that every person has three basic emotional needs: 1) someone to love, 2) someone to love you, and 3) somebody who understands or knows how you feel. Things like rejection, grief, insecurity, and self-centeredness can cause loneliness. Before my teens, I had already experienced three of these. As a child, I did not always have the luxury of managing grief. As a young person, I did not even realize rejection and insecurity made me feel isolated. Not having God in my life before high school, it is no wonder I sought relief in solitary, made-up games. How wonderful it would have been to know that Jesus knew how I felt.

By the time I was a successful entrepreneur, loneliness was so familiar to me that the internet, then social media, was my best friend. No wonder that by the time a holiday rolled around, I felt closed off from the rest of the real world. I felt alone in a crowded line of gift shoppers and not celebratory during July fireworks parties. But we celebrate Christmas because Jesus was God's gift of love to free us from sin and loneliness.

Jesus knows how I feel: "He was despised and rejected by mankind, a man of suffering, and familiar with pain. Like one from whom people hide their faces he was despised, and we held him in low esteem" (Isaiah 53:3, NIV). Jesus is the answer to my loneliness.

Unfortunately, the world offers attractive and tempting, but unsatisfying, alternatives to Jesus. This deception saddens me, knowing from experience that He comforts and is the one who understands.

Being More Social

Our society is ripe for isolation and rejection. We have never been more online social yet lonely. Exiting the airport on my way to Scottsdale Mall for a few last-minute Christmas gifts, I saw it everywhere. This solitary holiday season was a prime opportunity for the loneliness of millions. We shop online more and more, avoiding lines when possible. We hurry or unapologetically avoid conversation that delays getting to our next appointment. We wear earphones when working out and communicate through email and text messages. Online virtual books have turned a visit to the library into an archaic form of literary storage. Social media has all but annihilated the Christmas card via hand delivery or snail mail. Online FaceTime has superseded actual face-to-face time. The cell phone has made it hard to hold someone's attention in person over a meal.

In some situations, the other self-centered individual may as well not even be there. In his book *Fake*, Robert Kiyosaki asks, "Why is social media so anti-social?" and "How many times have you been talking to someone, and their body was there, but they were not?" This arrogance of pomposity has built up walls, and depersonalization has replaced common courtesy. Eye contact is a thing of the past, much less prayer before a meal holding hands. When someone is with you, half of the time it seems as if their mind is not. It is a good thing the Star Trek technology of the transporter is not a reality yet. It would separate us faster in a never-ending world of on-the-go self-satisfaction seekers. Home delivery for almost anything has removed the most basic in-person human interaction.

CHAPTER 5: HOLIDAY

The American Journal of Epidemiology published a study of 5,208 people in February 2017. They found the more time spent on social media, the more it had a detrimental impact. With increased time on social media came feelings of isolation, anxiety, and inadequacy. This replacement of personal interaction should never have been, and I did something about it when it came to my social media. I use my social media platforms for my photography business. Posting my work brings business and followers, and not doing so has the opposite effect. Yet once my relationship with Jenna entered a season of brokenness, all that changed, and I stopped posting. I became so tired of that fake, pretentious, and lonely world that I did not even look at my social media for months at a time.

Inevitably, when I would log on to answer a message, the first thing to pop up was an image of Jenna I wished I'd never seen. It only intensified the suffering and loneliness, resulting in longer durations of me ghosting social media. I may have missed out on income, but I have a new calling that involves interacting with real people in person. This practice helps to remove loneliness, fake relationships, and wasted time. God never intended for me to do life alone. I want real friendships, fellowship, and communication that involves interaction.

In June 2019, *The Wall Street Journal* reported that 35.7 million Americans live alone like me. In many cases, people live life alone on a sofa in front of a TV or computer each waking moment. Children play video games by themselves instead of catch or ball with others in the park or yard. Does anyone play in their yard anymore? People spend more time solo, looking down at the device in their hands than at the crosswalk ahead of them. Phone apps have taken away reality and replaced it with the best-animated version of almost everyone in my line of work.

Insecurity is no longer a problem unless you look in the mirror. Is anything or anyone real anymore? Has the twenty-first century ushered in the CGI era of humanity and interpersonal relations? Has our technology brought us closer together, or has it isolated us more than we realize? Has solitaire gone from a game to a way of life? Has there ever been a time in history when you can be in an airport terminal packed with people yet be ever so alone? Thank God I have found that the Lord is closer than I think through unwanted, lonely thoughts like this. He may be invisible, but His presence is everywhere: "The righteous cry out, and the Lord hears them; he delivers them from all their troubles" (Psalm 34:17, NIV).

I'm Not Forgotten

Walking through the splendor of Scottsdale Mall, often visited by the rich and famous, I saw a celebrity swagger. He was walking with a tall blonde wearing a form-fitting red dress, Gucci sunglasses, and a wide-brimmed hat to match. With his arm candy getting all the onlookers' attention, I wondered if he ever felt lonely. I have met quite a few famous people in my career who often experience loneliness. I was not alone in my loneliness, and some famous people have interesting things to say about that. Actor Robin Williams once said, "I used to think the worst thing in life was to end up all alone. It's not. The worst thing in life is to end up with people that make you feel all alone." A good friend has gone with me thrice over ten years to see her favorite singer, Mariah Carey, in concert. Perhaps Mariah sang it best when it comes to loneliness in her song "I Want To Know What Love Is."

I've learned that only God can fill an empty heart and give me the love I desire. And only God can give me the person who loves Him enough to deserve me. So rather than complaining when I'm lonely,

I now consider making it an opportunity to get to know God. No matter who has forgotten me, I'm always on God's mind.

When I'm lonely, which is more likely this time of year, there is music that speaks to my heart. It comes from one of my favorite artists, Amy Grant, in her song "Grown-up Christmas List." Her song narrates my grown-up Christmas wish.

When I need reminding that God has not forgotten me, I open my Bible for confirmation. God is intimately acquainted with all my ways according to Psalm 139:3, and He will provide my every need according to Philippians 4:19. His thoughts of me outnumber the grains of sand, according to Psalm 139:18. Nothing can separate me from God's love, according to Romans 8:38–39, and He will never leave me, according to Deuteronomy 31:6. He will be with me always, according to Matthew 28:20. I hope these encourage you as they do me.

God's My Comforter

As I approached my sister's store counter and prepared to greet her and all her enthusiastic department coworkers, I was not unaware of my true comforter. Yes, it is comforting to see family for Christmas and experience the good wishes of other friendly and familiar faces. The beautiful glitter and glamour of mall lighting and magnificent decorations are soothing to the weary soul. But nothing compares to the open arms of the God who comforts the lonely (see 2 Corinthians 1:3–4, Isaiah 51:12, and Matthew 5:4).

David, who wrote much of Psalms, was well acquainted with loneliness. Scholars refer to the prophet Jeremiah because of the difficulties he encountered as the "weeping prophet." Even Jesus, when on the cross, cried out, "My God, my God, why have you forsaken me?" (see Mark 15:34, NIV). I also know what it is like to feel abandoned by the person who mattered so much to me and how it leads to feeling lonely. And yet the Bible is full of inspiring words addressing loneliness. One of many verses on the subject is Deuteronomy 31:6 (NIV): "Be strong and courageous. Do not be afraid or terrified because of them, for the LORD your God goes with you; he will never leave you nor forsake you." My brokenness resulted in loneliness, so I connected with God and others.

I was not fine for a long time. I felt as though I was dying inside. I pretended everything was okay in front of others, but healing takes time. It may be contrary to popular belief, but time does not heal all wounds. God heals all wounds in time. Several things proved essential to recovering from my brokenness that will unfold through my story, but the cure for my lonely heart was Jesus alone and Him giving me a purpose.

God's with Me

After the Christmas holiday ended, it was time to head back home. Relaxing in my window seat on the return flight to California, my thoughts drifted into the past amid the soft, billowing clouds below. One resembled a musical instrument that was quite familiar to me. It reminded me of when I wrote and played a song on electric guitar for a girl I had dated when I was twenty-three years old. She was out of my league in appearance, class, and status. Her family dynamic with her parents and siblings was a picture of love and perfection.

Don't get me wrong; my mom was a saint in my eyes, and my stepdad was a devoted provider, although he ruled the home with a clenched fist. My stepdad sometimes lost his temper, dropping his fist on the dinner table with a loud thump that shook the tabletop and my nerves. It left the whole family in utter terror for the evening. Our family did not have prayer before meals; instead, it had an older sister who was often at odds with the family. My older sister would disrespect and argue with my mom or dad, requiring the other to step between them to keep the peace. My younger sister and I would often shrink back in the shadows, trembling inexorably inside. This girl's family interaction had something lacking at my house—family wholeness.

Dinner in their home sparked in me an early interest and desire for in-laws and extended family one day. It left me uninterested in photographing models for a season and more interested in securing a future family. I can still taste the buttery corn on the cob steaming in my mouth and hear her dad praying before our meal. This dad was the same one who unwittingly threw away my journal. Watching her kind, soft-spoken mom in the kitchen, with an apron on while serving dinner, was like viewing an old-school 1950s family. I can still picture where everyone sat at that table years ago, waiting for her pampering mom to join them before eating. For the first time, I saw family unity as a path leading away from a lonely future. I was all in! Her sisters adored me and communicated thrilling approval to their sibling for snagging a hot commodity like me. Not long after that dinner came the day of playing the song that I wrote for her. It touched her heart and brought tears to her eyes, but the relationship ended that day regardless. And there I was, alone again, not realizing that God was the only one still with me, no matter who left me. I never picked up my guitar again after that day, but my love for music never ceased.

Later in life, I filled my living room walls with twenty-nine electric guitars to prove that love to the world or to house guests. It was also a reminder to all who entered my home of my preferred hotel chain, the Hard Rock, and my love of music. One of my favorite performers back then was Amy Grant, and one of my most loved songs she sang was "Everywhere I Go." I saw her in concert at least seven different times during her prime. The lyrics to the song have resonated with me most of my life. If you have loved and lost and are still looking, you may be able to relate.

It took a long time for me to realize that God is the only one who will never leave me, as the song alludes. I hope it will comfort you to know that He is everywhere you go and will never leave you either. No matter who may abandon, betray, or leave me, He will never leave me. I am too precious to Him. His is the only divine love, and it is always there and available. "The LORD himself goes before you and will be with you; he will never leave you nor forsake you" (Deuteronomy 31:8, NIV). God is always with me everywhere I go.

Lonely's Final Thoughts

As my plane, with its clinking seatbelt notification and roar and then the rumble of the engines through the turbulence, made its final approach home after the holiday, I had some pervading thoughts. I recalled Jenna asking me more than once to play one of my electric guitars for her. Perhaps one day I will, after selecting the perfect song. Until then, I won't be in a hurry to get married, for it doesn't solve my loneliness problem. Instead, I'll leave all the picking and choosing up to God. My future spouse is not my loneliness cure. God cares for me and has a good plan for me. He understands my loneliness, so I socialize with others in ways that do not involve a screen. God knows how I feel and has not forgotten me. He is my true comforter. And most of all, God loves me and is always with me. His cure for loneliness is not having more friends in life or on social media. It's about having a purpose in life centered in Jesus Christ and why He willingly died on the cross.

"Turn to me and be gracious to me, for I am lonely and afflicted" (Psalm 25:16, NIV).

CHAPTER 6: WORSHIP

"David arose from the earth and washed and anointed himself and changed his clothes. And he went into the house of the Lord and worshiped" (2 Samuel 12:20, ESV).

Although a man after God's heart, David created his own worst nightmare. He turned from God and committed adultery with Bathsheba, and his sin led to the death of his innocent baby. But he arose and worshiped the Lord, seeking healing for his broken heart. Job lost it all, including his possessions and even his children. Still, he "arose and tore his robe and shaved his head and fell on the ground and worshiped" (Job 1:20, ESV).

I also know well the pain that comes with the frailty of a broken heart and the healing power of worshiping the Lord through it. Discovering through social media that Jenna had misled me was a crushing blow. Later, learning she was secretly and intimately involved with the same guy as suspected in Arizona was devastating. No message online or on TV could remove or sugarcoat the cold, hard facts of abandonment and deception. Her knowing how I felt about her after we developed a long, loyal relationship left a dagger's sting.

There was nothing in the medicine cabinet to treat this type of wound. It left an infection that spread from my pierced heart to my mindful imagination and broken spirit. I was tongue-tied with no words, thoughts, or ideas of what to do or say. The emotional and spiritual darkness around me was debilitating and seemingly impenetrable. It was during this time that I learned something amazing through a dream.

The Golden Room

After receiving God's message to do nothing about Jenna, it surprised me to find myself a recruit of seven bicyclists in another lucid dream. I woke up remembering it and will never forget what happened. Again, I do not usually remember dreaming, especially in vivid detail. So, I always know God is trying to tell me something when I remember them this way. In this second dream, the seven bicyclists were all mounted on shiny silver ten-speed bikes in single file. Each rider had gloves, protective clothing, a bicycle helmet, belts, gear, and dark glasses, even though it was evening. Their dark glasses were like shields and their gloves like swords. They wanted me to join them in riding around the city and protecting it, although no one spoke words to me. At night, they gave off a dazzling bright light against the darkness.

Before joining their group, I needed to go inside and retrieve my workout gloves. I thought of them as my boxing gloves in the dream for some reason. These gloves would protect me from the freezing chill and help me fight the enemy. When I entered the huge concrete edifice, I realized I had to go up before I could go in. I also noticed everything inside was gold, and I mean everything! This change was dramatic since everything in the dream until then had been in light or dark shades of gray.

Once inside the building, I had to go to the bathroom to relieve myself. I then realized every little thing in the restroom was gold, including the running water. Even the fluid flowing from my body as I relieved myself was liquid gold. Inside this place, which I felt was my home, I sensed a stranger hiding—a thief that I could not see in the dark. He took a bite of some fruit off a gold table, and it rolled onto the floor. I picked it up and put it back on the table with the jagged bite thrust from it. I then saw a woman who resembled my mom standing there, white like an angel but with short gray speckled hair. Startled, I suddenly woke up!

I started to ponder the meaning of this vision. It had to mean something special. God does not give us dreams and visions to frustrate us. It was only the second dream I had ever remembered after awakening. According to Genesis and Revelation, seven is God's number because it is perfect and complete. The seven bicyclists must have been from God. I doubt the angel was my mom. Although the angel resembled my mom, it did not look exactly like her. It must have been a trick.

Now, who deceives, breaks in and steals and also impersonates? It had to have been Satan disguised as an angel of light. "And no wonder, Satan himself masquerades as an angel of light" (2 Corinthians 11:14, BSB). My picking up the partially eaten fruit he had dropped must have represented something important. It appeared that I accepted his lies and disguises as good enough to be at the table of God's best for me. It seems God was reminding me of something: Until I had victory over Satan in private, God could not use me to my full potential in public. For God rewards people in public for what they do in private: "Your Father who sees in secret will reward you in public" (Matthew 6:6b, ABPE).

CHAPTER 6: WORSHIP

A couple of years before this dream, I was unaware that I was experiencing little sins that metastasized into complete defeat and compromise at Satan's hands. After about a year, I had improved. Since then, it has become a daily eradication. But not until I started a regular practice of what I discovered did I have victory. The more I sought God and all that He has to offer, the more the devil saw me as a threat and tried to break me down. As I resisted him, he fled from me. For as a child of God, "greater is he that is in you than he that is in the world" (1 John 4:4, KJV).

What was this monumental change that freed me from my past, pissed off the devil, and set me free? The answer is worship. If that sounds simple to you, think again. It took me a long time to get to this point—one little praise session was not what I needed to cure my aching heart. This tactic required a lifestyle change, but the results proved worth it. In my dream, those workout gloves represented my hands lifted in praise to God as I claimed His Word and fought off Satan. Sin no longer had its grip on me as in the past, which opened the floodgates for God to heal my broken heart. It was not something that happened overnight. Healing rarely is, and the heart is no exception. Referential worship of the Lord broke Satan's spell and grip on me after I discovered four things about it that helped it to heal me.

Worship Needed Prioritization

I, like David and Job, have my own worship stories. I was late to church again, which was getting so frustrating, but it wasn't intentional. It never became the priority it should have been until the season of brokenness over Jenna entered my life. What before was the warm-up sing-along before the sermon became much more to me—it became a resounding message. It blossomed into the priority it should have been all along. I'm not talking about church per se. I'm referring to the worship segment of church that starts the service or any gathering of believers.

Not until I learned the healing power of worship with others and on my own did my being late to take part in it end. Surrendering to the Lord in the name of Jesus in humble worship solved my "being late" problem. I'm sure that someone mentioned the benefits of worshiping the Lord to me at some point in the past. It is unfortunate, but it didn't resonate back then. Now that I know, I can't stress its importance enough as a part of my healing from heartbrokenness. It became so instrumental that I attended more than one church, one service right after the other. Sometimes I would even stay for the worship of the second service before driving to the next church so I could feel the Holy Spirit fill the room again. I not only received more teaching but double the worship portion as well.

The benefit of talented worship singers and musicians made the experience even better. The music and uplifting voices translated into an aura of quicker healing. The recordings I made of them on my phone continued to be a blessing wherever I traveled with my earphones. There's no way to explain it—you would have to experience it yourself to know what I mean. "The fact that God has blessed us with His favor when we deserve His wrath fades from our memories like a song whose lyrics we once knew but now cannot recall," says Paul David Tripp in *New Morning Mercies*. It took a long time, but I finally got what all the fuss was about when it came to worship. I now understood why worship was such a big part of David's writings in Psalms. "Praise the LORD with the harp; make music to him on the ten-stringed lyre" (Psalm 33:2, NIV).

Worship has become one of the core things I now do as a believer. I fought sorrow and depression by doing my part and allowing God to do His part. My role was to call upon the Lord in praise and thankful worship, submitting my will to the Lord for help. Through the Holy Spirit's power, He started healing my broken heart and freed me from depression and fear. As I clung to the steadfast love of the Lord and knelt before Him, I lifted my hands and heart in praise to the Lord in the name of Jesus as I spoke His Word back to Him. I praised Him as my rock, fortress, and deliverer. He became my shield and strength, the one in whom I could trust and take refuge, as it says in Psalm 144:1–2. I let Him fight for me.

Turning my worry into worship, I watched God turn my brokenness into blessings. Satan wanted to drag me down into the foreboding pit of depression and despair, so I let God move on my behalf as I prioritized worshiping Him.

Worship Was Hard

I did not receive fair treatment but felt misled, abandoned, and betrayed by my best friend. I felt as though my broken story might never end and believed worshiping through it would be hard. But I found it important to worship the Lord not only in good times but through difficult times as well. I discovered that I needed to worship God and His magnificence not because life is good but because He is good. I've heard that when we worship God, we join with choirs of angels that bow before God's throne in continuous praise. Although we cannot hear their voices, our praise is as distinct and audible in heaven. So I joined God's angels in worship, even in the midst of my troubles, and released my cares to Him in praise, fearing Him rather than my situation.

The Lord takes pleasure and delights in those who worship Him in reverence and fear (see Psalm 147:11). I discovered that when I would worship the Lord in reverential awe, He would remove my fear of people and move on my behalf: "The LORD will grant that the enemies who rise up against you will be defeated before you. They will come at you from one direction but flee from you in seven" (Deuteronomy 28:7, NIV). God loves justice and hates wrongdoing. In the end, He could bring justice to my situation, so I let Him be my vindicator while I worshiped Him with reverent fear and gratitude, even though it was hard.

At first, worshiping was the last thing I wanted to do. I was already suffering. In the natural, adding a task to my emotional pain by bearing down on my knees or lifting my arms to worship seemed unappealing. Who does this through suffering anyway? My path was already laden with tears and toil. Did I even have a reason or need to offer God praise and worship at a time that seemed so hard? I could not have been more wrong. It may have been hard at times, but it was worth it, and there was a good reason.

I thought of Jesus, who experienced a brutal beating that disfigured His face and whipping that tore the flesh from his back. I've cringed from the finger prick of a rose stem thorn, yet Jesus wore a crown of thorns that dug into His brow and nails that pierced through His hands and feet. He hung on a cross, thighs pushing and feet pressing against those nails for every breath to prevent suffocation for six hours. I do not know the meaning of hard compared to Jesus. How could I complain about how hard it may be to spend a little time each day in humble worship of Him after all He did for me? I had a lot of pain to complain about, but no matter how hard worship was, I worshiped anyway. No one knows hard like Jesus, and yet He never complained.

Despite my tear-stained path, I praised God for all I could be grateful for enduring. I found many reasons to praise the Lord. Lifting thankful praise unto the Lord as a weeping worshiper transformed my despair into hope and joy that didn't depend on my circumstances. I found gratitude to be a vital step on the road to healing. I worshiped the Lord through my problems and let Him mend me. I don't know precisely why worshiping God has the power to heal a broken heart. I only know that it does. And that led to my next discovery.

Worship Heals Hearts

I did not feel like it at the time, but my wounded heart was primed for worship. Talking about past mistakes or thinking about what I didn't want brought more of what I didn't want. Always contemplating what was wrong with my life only gave me more of what was wrong. Praise and worship instead took my mind off my problems. This removal of my cares and worries allowed me to focus on God and receive His healing. It took focusing on how much Jesus loved me—enough to suffer and die for me. Mindful praise and worship of the Lord on my knees turned my focus away from Jenna and placed it on God. It removed my conscious mind from problems as I lifted my broken heart and placed it into God's healing hands.

I thought I was too weak and brokenhearted to worship. But without praise and worship, I had little power greater than myself to face despair alone. I knew in my mind I was never alone with the Lord on my side, but worshiping Him is what renewed my strength and healed my broken heart. I found it even more critical when I felt broken than when feeling well. Healing through worshiping God was a momentous discovery for me.

Worship Has Protocol

I thought I understood worship until I learned how to receive God's healing from it. It was all in my posture. I would get down on my knees and lift my hands. Sometimes I would even bow down to show God humility and respect. It was an outward display of the attitude within me. The devil couldn't see what was in my heart and couldn't read my mind, but he could see me on my knees, lifting my hands in worship to God. He knew what was going on. He could see he was losing the battle, which made him afraid because he wanted me to stay broken inside. I scheduled time to be alone with God each day, repeating this prayer aloud throughout my day: "Lord, heal my heart, restore my soul, and make me whole." When necessary, I whispered it.

In the beginning, having learned this from best-selling author and ministry leader Terri Savelle Foy, I asked myself, *Does this really work?* I would not be sharing this if I had only heard or read it and not actually experienced it. I remember so many nights coming home late from work, tired and broken inside, just like Terri. But having scheduled or planned time before going to bed to worship the Lord, I did so.

At first, it was hard to start. I had to force myself. I would brood, *How can I praise and worship God when I feel so hurt and abandoned by Him and Jenna?* I would also think, *No one is ever going to know that I spent night after night on my knees in the dark in front of the stereo. Does anyone else sing along with worship music like this? Does lifting my hands and voice to the Lord in humble words of praise and worship make a difference?* Other than my cats, who would often be near my side waiting for attention or bedtime, no one knew what I was doing. If anyone did ever find out what I was doing, then what? The devil would whisper in my ear, "They are going to think you are crazy or insecure." But I would press on with my knees hurting at times and always with tears streaming down my face.

I can remember my heart feeling like it would burst out of my chest. The gripping pain of sorrow over Jenna clung as dripping tears fell from my chin. But through it all, the peaceful healing of God through the Holy Spirit comforted my spirit. His angels surrounded me with protection: "God will command his angels to protect you wherever you go" (Psalm 91:11, CEV). Praise had the power to lighten the massive load of pain I was carrying. God invited me to bring my laments to Him so He could turn my hopelessness and brokenness into praise: "Taste and see that the Lord is good" (Psalm 34:8, NIV). Even as I write this chapter, I have praise music on pause. I plan to be on my knees again tonight after getting discouraging news about Jenna this very day. The Lord became my fortress and God the rock in whom I would take refuge.

I cannot tell you how many thousands of times I have asked the Lord to "heal my heart, restore my soul, and make me whole." Over and over in the car or at the gym, I spoke the words. While on a walk, during a bike ride, or while showering, I have done this with regularity. I have even mouthed it underwater while swimming laps. And, of course, I have done this on my knees in prayer or lying in bed night after night. Many nights, it was with tears running down my face during long, difficult times.

After a while, my words changed. Without realizing the difference, I started saying, "Thank you, Lord, for healing my heart, restoring my soul, and making me whole." It was a subtle difference but a psychological one as well as spiritual. Before I knew it, I had peace and felt what I was saying, even though my situation had not yet changed. Getting alone with the Lord in worship to seek Him as the healer of my heart and receiving the love of God was key to my healing. God was pouring His love into my heart so that I could experience healing from the inside out.

I found that praising and thanking God was a way to receive His love. So I praised Him not for what I was going through but because of what He one day would do. I would turn off my phone and the TV to be alone with God. I would raise my hands and say, "God, I receive Your love for me," and tell Him how I felt. I asked Him to fill me with His love. Without realizing it, I was opening the windows and floodgates of heaven. This method of worship caused God to start pouring that love into me. Receiving God's love is the medicine that heals a broken heart. So worship is what I did when hurting—especially while I was hurting.

After learning this from Terri, I practiced it when I had so much pain in my heart because of Jenna. After Aslan's passing, it became a nightly thing for me. Sometimes, Kira would run down the stairs, whizzing past and jumping over my feet as I knelt to the worship music. Other times, she would meow from upstairs. Either way, she knew bedtime and hugs followed worship and prayer. God used worship to turn a mess into a message for Terri and now for me.

Final Worshiping Thoughts

I would never have chosen this course if I controlled the joystick in this game of love and life. But thank God, He used worrying, suffering, and loneliness to lead me to worship. For I know the pain that comes with a broken heart, and now I know the healing power of worshiping the Lord through it. It's sometimes physically demanding to get down on my knees when tired or achy and emotionally grueling when sadness is overwhelming, but worship is now a priority. I can now fight sorrow and depression by doing my part and allowing God to do His. As I worship the Lord through problems, I fear Him, not my situation, for God is my vindicator. I will never be too weak and brokenhearted to worship and receive God's medication—His never-ending love. And that's no hyperbole.

> "Worship the Lord your God, and his blessing will be on your food and water. I will take sickness from among you" (Exodus 23:25, NIV).

CHAPTER 7: GOOD

"And let us not lose heart in doing good, for in due time we shall reap if we do not grow weary. So then, while we have opportunity, let us do good to all men, and especially to those who are of the household of the faith" (Galatians 6:9–10, NASB1977).

*N*ever did I imagine doing this kind of job. I had a full-time career running my own company and was always busy. Moreover, I rarely worked less than sixty hours per week. Nevertheless, taking on a new commitment, a second job I had never trained or studied for, was not a fear of mine. But it was not my primary focus either. Agreeing to take on this extra work for my longtime friend's company under the auspices as a bartender would take two or three evenings per week, but doing so for Makara (her name meaning "pharaoh's daughter") was an easy decision. Adding it to my schedule while continuing my own established career did not worry me. The fact that it was in the evening, when people usually relax, go out with friends, or date, didn't matter either. Knowing that it would cut into hours I usually saved to run my company did

CHAPTER 7: GOOD

not sway my decision. The piling up of unfinished work was only an afterthought.

Working for Makara's company as a volunteer without pay did not deter me. Reimbursement for gas to the job did not cross my mind. Makara bought me dinner on most nights I worked, but a meal does not pay the bills. My services were rendered free based on friendship. No tips for me—they all went to Makara or Jenna. Yes, Jenna. The greatest gift someone can give is to lay their life down for a friend. This sacrifice of time and labor was much easier than that.

However, learning the skill of a new job I had no practical use for looked pointless at first. Performing free manual labor each week only for the benefit of others seemed a little absurd. Only two things mattered: I was helping a longtime friend's company while covering Jenna's shift. If I didn't, Jenna would lose her job while away for a season (even though she didn't realize I was covering for her). After she returned, I continued to cover for her when she could not come in, regardless of my schedule or plans. This hardship ensured Jenna would not lose her shift during the best part of her future work schedule. Some of the most meaningful gifts you can give others are acts of kindness they can never repay. They are undoubtedly rewarding, especially if they come at the high cost of hardship over extended periods.

Why was Jenna gone for a season? She was living out of town, dating the guy I had confronted her about in Arizona. Then why in the world did I cover for her? This question is the one asked of me many times by the only other two people who knew. God put this desire in my heart for several reasons, but here are a few.

The Bible says that doing good for others who hurt you can bring *you* a blessing (see 1 Peter 3:9). It was also the right and honorable thing to do (see Romans 12:17). It fulfilled the command Jesus gave in Luke 6:31 of doing for others as you would have them do for you. In simple terms, it prevented Makara from losing her business, for one weekend night without Jenna there or me to cover for her could cost the business thousands. That was reason enough. If these reasons are still hard to swallow, consider the benefits I found in doing good.

The Restroom Lesson

I recall one night, a couple of months into this job, when I had worked for seven hours till almost midnight. I had completed all my tasks, including stocking, organizing, and doing paperwork. I finished preparations for the employees coming in the next day and was ready to retire for the night. That quickly changed when I was alone with Makara, the company owner, and we discovered that the women's restroom had flooded. There was no discussion. I simply got the mop and bucket, then proceeded to spend the next twenty minutes wondering about God's purpose in all this. I had become the free bathroom janitor saddled with much to contemplate.

So trust me when I say I understand emotional brokenness. My arms and back hurt much less than my broken heart through the drudgery of that experience. And it had nothing to do with the fact I was doing all this as a volunteer, even though my first thought was that this wasn't what I signed up for. The pain was emanating from the knowledge that Jenna, whose shift I was covering, would never know. She would never hear about this one little experience of many I endured so she could keep her job, so no one would ever question her insouciance. I never in my wildest imagination dreamed I would be writing about this in a book at the time. I assumed the only reward for my travails would come from God giving me a twofold recompense for all that I had suffered in shame (see Isaiah 61:7), and I had no idea when in the future that might come.

I knew what was going on inside of me while in that restroom. It was no coincidence that it was the women's restroom. I did not realize it at the time, but God was smoothing over my character like sandpaper. Under my breath, I claimed my most comforting Bible verse, Psalm 34:18 (NIV), a year before I would also need it for Aslan: "The Lord is close to the brokenhearted and saves those who are crushed in spirit." I whispered over and over, "God, I don't understand the purpose of going through all this. But I trust that you will make a way when there seems to be no way" (see Isaiah 43:16). I repeated these words again and again, weeping in silence. I wiped the tears away with my forearm while squeezing the dirty water from the mop into the bucket. Back then, I did not grasp to its full extent what I will share with you now. Everything I was going through was preparing me for that which I had requested. Plus, if God can make a way through the wilderness, rivers, and deserts, He can make a way for me (see Isaiah 43:19). This incident also showed me that you don't fight fire with fire; you fight fire with water. One of my deadliest enemies of living a life of doing good was the pursuit of future comfort, and the fire of that pursuit needed dousing. I would rather choose to help over doing nothing any day anyway.

My Secret Pain

I found myself feeling weighed down by a plethora of problems. Life seemed unfair. I felt like God was punishing me even though I was doing the right thing. Why was God allowing this, and why couldn't I understand His intentions? I needed to begin thinking and saying the right thing before it happened. In the midst of my pain, I needed to call upon those things that are not as though they were, as it says in Romans 4:17. I knew God loved me and had a good plan for me. I trusted that He would make the wrong things in my life right while I was doing good for others. This belief required me to think of others and not only myself. This selfless attitude made it easier to do good and not focus on my problems. I had to seek God's presence rather than only His gifts. I needed to seek the Lord in humility and bring my concerns and petitions to the one who saw my secret pain. You know precisely the kind of discomfort I mean. We hide it behind the masked response we often display to people who ask, "How are you doing?" If you are typical, like me, your reply is, "Oh, I'm good."

Ever been there? Yes, we *all* have! I had to learn to submit to God willingly amid adverse circumstances. I did this by focusing on God rather than the problem. I knew His reward for seeking Him through this: "Take delight in the LORD, and he will give you the desires of your heart" (Psalm 37:4, NIV). Focusing on God and His future reward is what I did whenever working for my friend for free. I sought the Lord and worked as if working for Him: "Whatever you do, work at it with all your heart, as working for the Lord, not for human masters" (Colossians 3:23, NIV).

Leaning on God

I had no idea what I was in for with this side job. "Michael, one of the other bartenders, is sick. Can you work a double shift for me on Sunday?" asked Makara Saturday night. "Ah, what are you talking about, Miquel? Give it to me," the cook berated with an unsavory snarl. "Tell your customer that's how you cook a steak." And "No, no, no. You serve it like this and open it like that," said the *maître d'*. "Michael, don't forget an Old-Fashioned needs a couple of dashes of bitters, and remember to use the copper cups for a Moscow Mule," said the other bartender over the gaggle of women sitting at the bar. "Make that martini extra dirty," an impertinent customer ordered.

What in the world does that mean? It sounds gross, were my thoughts the first time I heard that request, and nothing changed my mind when I found out what it meant. *Sweet or sour vermouth with a Manhattan?* I asked myself early on while the cascading drink orders outpaced my fastidious ability to ring them up. "Michael, can you wipe down all the tables and put the chairs up before we close?" Makara asked while I took out the trash and empty bottles before stocking the wine rack. Then my phone lit up for a moment behind the bar. "Michael, can you edit some extra pictures for me ASAP?"

Later that night, a voicemail, "I need a shoot. When is your soonest opening?" Then, right as I finished cleaning all the martini glasses, a slew of loud patrons walked in the door for one last round before we closed. *This is not even my real job,* I thought. I had reached exhaustion, but the fatigue could not overcome my desire to lean on the Lord. Then my phone lit up again. "I need your advice, Michael. Please call me." It was not uncommon for women to ventilate with melancholy their cascade of urgent problems to me at any time of day and with no regard to my schedule. And behind the counter, I served the occasional bombastic, silver-tongued, manipulative, and portentous types of men I had heard about from these women.

I felt overwhelmed by everything I was going through and supposed to be doing. Solomon seemed to have similar feelings, as recorded in 2 Chronicles. Solomon sought God for wisdom, and God gave it to Him (see 2 Chronicles 1:9–10). I, too, wanted to learn to make wise choices by seeking God's wisdom, especially through my complex and uncertain situation with Jenna. God closed the lions' mouths for Daniel, parted the Red Sea for Moses, and made the sun stand still for Joshua. He put a baby in Sarah's womb and raised Lazarus from the dead. If He can do all that, He can take care of me. Nothing I was facing was too hard for Him to handle, so I allowed God to take care of and guide me while I did good things for others. I trusted God would lead me to navigate through my broken circumstances by leaning on Him. Working for Makara was no exception.

The Unexpected Good

One night, while assisting a middle-aged couple at Makara's company, something unexpected and life-changing happened. I had never experienced something that required wisdom beyond mine with such quick action. The husband of the couple I was assisting started to choke on something he was eating in my presence. No one was closer to the couple than I was. I sensed all eyes in the building fixated on the situation. Everyone remained frozen in their tracks as he stood up, gasping to breathe. There was a long, silent pause—the kind that makes you wish somebody were scratching a blackboard instead to fill the eerie emptiness. The enormity of the moment did not go unnoticed by me. It looked as if it were up to me. In an instant, I knew God had put me in this place for a reason. I stood behind the man and pulled in, attempting the Heimlich maneuver. I had only seen it on TV and had never tried it myself. His large, heavy-set frame made it difficult to reach around him.

The first attempt was unsuccessful. My heart pounding was the loudest sound in a rapt room of stunned silence. It was like trying to dance with armor strapped on—bulky and awkward. I could see the shock and helpless terror on his wife's face and open mouth as she glanced at me like one of those slow-motion scenes in a hospital drama. The terror in her eyes sat like a boulder in my throat. *Oh no. I need a miracle, God*, was all my brain could conjure in that harrowing moment of adrenaline pumping through my veins. Without much hesitation, I did it a second time, this time much harder. The man coughed and spat out something onto the floor, able to breathe normally again. The sigh of relief and handclapping filled the air. You could not only feel the emotion; you could hear it. The ecstatic and grateful man, who was hearty in his approbation and lavish in his praise—thank you, Dale Carnegie—handed me a large tip he insisted I take before leaving. That whole week, the talk was that I had saved his life. But the truth was that God had saved his life. I was only an available vessel used by God for good.

But the incident did remind me that it's not all about me. Sometimes, God puts us in situations to help others when they need it the most and when we least expect it. Would this man have lived if God had not called me to volunteer at Makara's company for Jenna? To elevate beyond my brokenness, I needed to set aside my self-centeredness. I had to realize that there are other hurting people in this world. Many of them may benefit from and appreciate someone being there for them in their time of need.

Working for Makara, I encouraged someone else who was hurting inside. I met a close friend of Makara's at her business whom she treated to dinner and drinks to comfort him. He had buried his wife that day, and I sensed God drawing me to encourage him. I found him alone for a moment and stood close to him. I asked if he could give me some advice on how he managed to stay married for fifty-eight years to the same person. I listened, waiting for the right moment to share anything God might want me to say. He talked for a while, revealing to me some very personal information. He also was very gracious in crediting his Catholic wife, who believed in only one marriage for life. My genuine interest and caring appeared to do some good for him. In the end, I told him a little about the book I was starting to write and how I would ensure he got a copy when it was all done. He cracked a smile, and I felt a bit better as well.

Good Builds Confidence

Giving my life away by doing good for others was beneficial for my confidence. You may not have been expecting that breaking news, but I can testify from experience that it is true. Plenty of self-help books promote taking care of yourself and making you the center of everything. Their main goal is for you to become self-sufficient and confident. So stand tall and keep your shoulders straight and your chin up. But remember, life is not all about you. I concur with Tim Tebow, who expressed a similar thought in *Mission Possible*: "One of the greatest questions you can ask yourself is, Does my life change other people's lives for the better?"

Real confidence comes from knowing the one who loved you enough to die for you. It grows by giving your life away to others for His sake. God wanted me healed and made whole so that I could walk out the plan for my life. Part of that plan was doing good for others in need. While I was hurting, God wanted to use me to help someone else, so I let Him. And being a blessing to others grew my confidence as I relied on God rather than myself.

Good Through Pain

Sitting around doing nothing while suffering inside did not make my problem disappear. It was not easy or natural to set out to do good things for others when I was craving help myself. I was trying to put the pieces back together in my own heart and soul. I asked myself, *How is this going to help me?* I felt like a broken record, detached from my unplugged phonograph. No one wanted to play my song anymore, so why should I go out and make music for others? Looking in the mirror, I could see someone discarded as beyond repair. But as a doer of good, I became more like a zealous lighthouse of hope for others. For those beyond broken themselves to reach me, I needed to be portable, like a Coast Guard vessel.

I couldn't spend all my time inside my own little safe harbor of calm waters tied to the dock. I best set sail for deeper waters, where I would meet others in need, like Makara. That is where I met the healing waters of doing good as I rescued other broken vessels like myself. Do you think it was exciting working for free three nights a week, month after month, for two years? Do you think I enjoyed shutting down my own business twenty hours a week to slave over someone else's company? Do you think it was fun to cheerfully cover for Jenna every week, knowing she was with someone else in the meantime? It was an epic physical and emotional task, stretching the elasticity of my mind, especially at first. But after a while, I came to enjoy then crave the opportunity to serve and help others with no apparent benefit to me. I found that there were few things as rewarding or healing as doing good for others who couldn't repay me. I also understood why the gregarious and sometimes adorably pretentious Jenna liked the attention of this spotlight behind the bar.

When contemplating right or wrong, I used to think in simple terms like *Did I do anything wrong today?* The real question should be, *Did I do anything good today?* Many people don't feel passionate about anything, so they don't do anything. If they pray, they do so only if they need something that's out of their control. Getting out of their broken situation is an example. Even some Christians I know don't attend church if they don't feel like it. When they do, they praise the Lord during worship only if they feel like it. And they don't worship on their own in the privacy of their homes. They read their Bibles, but only if they have the time and energy.

How do I know this beyond my Sunday observation? Because I used to be like that too. But that was not God's way or will for my life after practicing Matthew 6:33. And as a result, doing good with zeal became a natural part of my daily life. It was like exercise. I didn't want to go to the gym and work out sometimes, especially in the beginning. But the more I exercised, the easier it got, and the better I felt. Doing good was a positive exercise that made me feel good on the inside, even though my pain lingered.

Final Good Thoughts

The most meaningful gifts I've given others are acts of kindness they can never repay. They were rewarding, though, especially when they came at a high cost emotionally. Like smores over a campfire, doing good for Jenna melted my heart toward God even when she was unaware or did not care. Doing good for someone else amid my pain was the right and honorable thing to do. It blessed Makara and her many customers, and it kept Jenna from getting fired. Everything I went through working for her was preparing me for what I requested of God. I know He will make the wrong things in my life right because I have done good for others. As I have leaned on God, He has led me through my broken circumstances. And no matter what lies ahead in my journey of doing good, I know the Lord will be there through every hurdle and hardship. He will carry me through life's valleys and celebrate with me through the peaks.

There are other hurting people in this world, like Makara, her choking customer, and some of the many patrons I humbly served for her with love and tenderness. I came to enjoy and now look back with fondness on those God allowed me to wait on without them knowing I did it for free. I hope my story will benefit some of them in their time of need. Until then, I will continue to do good and let God do the rest.

"And let us consider how to stimulate one another to love and good deeds" (Hebrews 10:24, LSB).

CHAPTER 8: TRUST

"Trust in the Lord and do good" (Psalm 37:3, NIV).

"*D*o you have time to help today?" Little did I know what my volunteering to help Jenna's sister (who we will call "Whitney") and her family move would mean. Whitney is the sister whose new home Jenna would later invite me to go with her to for Thanksgiving. The "move from" address was the same street and complex where my sister and her husband once lived. The "move to" street address was a block away from my old junior high school. More items needing moving were at a storage facility across the street from my first job. What are the chances of all that having a connection?

If I have not intimated it by now, let me do so plainly here. God knows the end of our story from the beginning. There are no such things as coincidences. "Coincidences" are God's humorous way of letting us know that He's got it all under control so we can trust Him. Drive after drive for weeks on end was not enough. I lost track of how many trips up and down stairs with boxes and furniture in hand this move required. Loading and unloading SUVs was so frequent it felt like a part-time job. I became the mighty volunteer U-Haul go-to guy and had no problem with it. Why? Even though

I assumed the real one I was doing this for might never know how I went out of my way to help her sister, God would know. Nothing goes unseen by God, and He is a rewarder of those who seek Him with diligence (see Hebrews 11:6).

Trusting God and doing good was one way I was demonstrating that belief. It was a pleasure and honor to go out of my way; to help the people I treated as family. Even if Whitney never ended up as my sister-in-law, she would always be my sister in the Lord. Doing good was the easy and natural part—the trusting component was another thing. It took repeated acts of kindness toward this family rather than a one-time assist to get the job done. The consistency of action helped them and increased my trust in the Lord at the same time.

Seeking freedom from my brokenness led me to seek opportunities to bless others, which, in turn, blessed me. "To have a blessing you must be broken. It is the price you must pay to get there," says Pastor Paula White Cain. Doing good works for others helped heal my wounded soul and demonstrated my trust in God. It got my mind off myself and my problems. I had so many troubles that left me bemused. I couldn't afford to pass up the opportunity to help. I just had to believe that God would find a way to bless me if I trusted Him and did good. When you cannot be repaid or accept only friendship as payment, the blessing is even greater. I did not experience trust in God like I could until I helped someone who could not repay me. Trusting God and doing good needed to be part of my life, but the first thing it required was not knowing.

Trusting Without Knowing

Trust requires not knowing God's plan, so I needed to trust the One who knew the answers to all my problems rather than needing to know it all myself. I didn't understand what was happening in my life, and I needed to be fine with that. I needed to step out in faith and trust God to handle it rather than trying to figure it out myself. The Bible never once says, "Figure it out," but over and over, it says, "Trust God." He's already figured it out. God wasn't asking me to figure it out. He was asking me to trust that He already had. I did not know the full scope of what Jenna was doing while out of town for weeks as I helped her sister, but God knew, and He had a plan.

I had to trust God while not knowing while hurting and waiting. Through these experiences, I learned to trust that God had a plan. And no matter how uncertain my path may look, God has a good plan for my life and is in control. In every situation, there are two versions: the version I can see and the version God sees.

I also learned that God stops working if I take over and try to handle it myself. So I placed my problem in His hands, giving Him back control, and trusted Him to manage it for me. Doing this did not mean I stopped praying or thanking Him that He had control over the situation. It only meant releasing power back to Him. God gives us things we can't handle so we can learn to rely on Him to handle them. Those who leave everything in God's hands eventually see God's hands in everything.

I spent thousands of hours listening to Bible teaching and read dozens of books to help mend my heart and get God's guidance for my life. I searched high and low for solutions to brokenness. The answer was much less complicated than I first thought; I do not have to listen to every lie that Satan screams in my ear. I can say, "I don't have to know!" God has a plan, and it is better than mine. And guess what? He's not telling, at least not at the moment.

I learned one crucial thing: The answer to all my problems is to trust God and do good. I found incredible power and relief from despair through prayer and worship with thanksgiving. And yes, there is blessing and healing in fellowship and the comforting words of the Bible. But I found that there is nothing like trusting God and doing good while He is solving your problem.

Trusting that God would take care of my problem brought great relief. It relieved the misery of worry, fear, and headache from thinking about my situation constantly. Knowing God is in control and that He is in charge is a very freeing sensation. Trusting God freed me from trying to do what I could not do. It released me from the need to figure everything out. Why does this matter? Because even when I thought I had the answer, I still didn't have it. But God did, and His way was better than mine.

There will come a time in my life when I know everything, but it is not now. If I trust God regardless, I can go through life not knowing many things and still be content and at peace. I can still hear Joyce Meyer as if it were yesterday saying these same things as I listened to her repeatedly until it became ingrained in my mind. Her voice was a constant reminder to trust God even while not knowing His plan as I waited for news from Jenna.

Trying vs. Trusting

Trusting required me to leave my concerns in God's hands. This kind of trust meant not going on Facebook for two years or posting any of my work on my business Instagram any longer, reading my Bible instead. Life became more real and spiritually uplifting without social media. But trusting God and casting my cares on Him required that I decide to do so. I was trying to trust God but was still worried and feeling anxious. I also stopped adding my photography to all of my websites and was initially nervous, but it did not slow down my business. God wanted me to stop trying and start trusting. Doing so changed everything, but it meant applying God's Word. Instead of trying to fix the wrong areas of my business and my life with Jenna, I trusted God to help me separate the good and evil in my business while trusting Him to care for Jenna.

Psalm 115:11 (NLT) reminds us, "…trust in the LORD! He is your helper and your shield." I had to trust in, lean on, rely on, and have confidence in God. He is my refuge: "The LORD is my rock, my fortress, and my deliverer. My God is my rock, in whom I take refuge, my shield and the horn of my salvation, my stronghold" (Psalm 18:2, BSB). And God will shelter me if I put my trust in Him: "This I declare about the LORD: He alone is my refuge, my place of safety; he is my God, and I trust him" (Psalm 91:2, NLT).

I left my concerns about what Jenna was up to in God's hands. I trusted Him that she would contact me when she needed me, as usual. And if she never did, God was equipping me to be ready either way. I was not worrying or trying to trust—I was going about my business, leaving it up to God.

God's Equipping Me

My broken cries of help from hurt and worry were not an unfamiliar sound to God. He has heard it before. David wrote of his pain long before I came along: "For I am poor and needy, and my heart is wounded within me" (Psalm 109:22, NIV). Still, David trusted God to take care of his problems: "For he stands at the right hand of the needy, to save their lives from those who would condemn them" (Psalm 109:31, NIV). If David could trust God to save him from death, I could trust God to get me through my broken situation. God was using my pain to equip me to help other hurting people. I learned that God loves using people who have been hurt and broken then healed. Why? No person can comfort as well as one who has had the same problem or injury as those they are trying to help.

God was equipping me to help others and come to Him first. "God can take your brokenness and mend your pain. Your pain becomes your platform. God does His finest work in the lives of broken people," says Paula White Cain. The loving help of others was nice, but I could not replace going to God with going to others. It would only weaken my trust in God. God wanted me stable, with no weak spots in my life. The more I depended on and went to Him first, the more He did for and through me to help others. Brokenness allowed me to receive some of God's greatest blessings, but it required me to trust that God was preparing me.

Waiting for Justice

When I had difficulty trusting God, it was comforting to know that He is just. That meant He would always make the wrong things in my life right in the end. I only needed to trust that He would do so in His way and timing. Life is not fair, but God is just. So I placed my trust in Him, releasing the burden of my problems. I had to trust that He would bring justice to my situation if I gave Him control. And by justice, I mean future blessing to me and loving revelation to Jenna. Trusting God for justice removed my need to try to do it myself. God says in the Bible, "'Vengeance is Mine, I will repay,' says the Lord" (Romans 12:19, NASB).

To experience that kind of justice, I had to turn the problem over to God and not try to manage it myself. Releasing it to God without interfering was hard at first and a constant struggle. Trusting God was difficult because He did not grant my request immediately. I had to wait for freedom from the bondage of pain through over four years of suffering because of Jenna's back-and-forth entering and exiting my life. This seesaw required me to envision God manifesting justice in my life before resolution with Jenna rather than simply trusting Him for it after. But God often does some of His best work in our waiting, and it taught me to trust Him more, building my faith while developing my patience.

The waiting part was a test that strengthened my faith, requiring me not to give up because the wait was longer than I expected. I was hurting, but I trusted God to be with and help me: "Never will I leave you; never will I forsake you" (Hebrews 13:5, NIV).

Trust Breeds Confidence

I was a brokenhearted mess on the mend, needing hope in something more powerful than myself. As a Christian, my confidence should have been in Jesus. After placing my trust in God, I became more confident with my situation because I know He is trustworthy. Trust then freed me from stress, worry, and fear.

My confidence grew even when I didn't feel very confident because my trust was growing in God. My feelings changed without warning, so I could not place my confidence in how I felt. But with faith in God, I could trust Him to give me favor. "The LORD bestows favor and honor; no good thing does he withhold from those whose walk is blameless. LORD Almighty, blessed is he who trusts in you" (Psalm 84:11–12, NIV). The evil one did not want me to have confidence because he knew I wouldn't achieve much in life if I lacked it.

God Handles Best

God wanted to help me through my brokenness, but as long as I was trying to fix my problem myself, He wouldn't force me to accept His help. God also provided support and encouragement through a friend—an invaluable relationship. She was often there with a word of womanly wisdom, an uplifting scripture, a listening ear, and prayer together. God expected me to trust Him but was always ready and available to handle anything I could not.

I need to point out that "God won't give you more than you can handle" is not a Bible verse. When a problem arises in our lives, this supposed verse gets tossed about like a Scripture bomb. Sure, it sounds compelling, and it is a reminder of God's care and concern. After all, He knows the exact number of hairs growing out of my head (see Luke 12:7). But it's because God loves me and knows me so well that He had to give me more than I could handle. After all, I tended to think that I could do everything on my own.

Thinking this way was a form of pride, and it was dragging me down (see Proverbs 16:18). To keep me trusting in my need for a savior, God allowed me to see how much I couldn't handle. Now, the Bible does say that God won't allow us to be "tempted" beyond our limits (see 1 Corinthians 10:13), but "temptation" is not the problem I am referring to here. God wanted me to trust Him. It is logical, then, to conclude that I can expect situations I can't control to develop that trust.

This kind of situation is just what happened to me while only communicating with Jenna's sister for weeks and never about Jenna. Whitney's frequent texts asking for my help with her moving if I had time and was sure it was okay were sweet. Our conversation and teamwork working on her project focused on the job at hand, her children, husband, and parents, not her sister. Her thankyous and hugs were many and heartfelt. One thing is for sure—I have a lot more confidence now that the Lord will handle it than I did then. I trust God to help me do my best and trust Him to do the rest.

God Knows Best

Trust means acknowledging God knows best. Admitting that meant I understood that God knows better than I do. But it was my choice to recognize that fact or continue to wonder and worry about Jenna, even while helping her sister. God not only wanted me to trust Him but expected it.

My fear of not getting what I wanted was the real cause of my reluctance to trust God fully. I thought that the only way I could be sure of getting what I wanted with this relationship was by taking care of it myself. But that fear prevented me from completely trusting God. I needed to believe that God always had my best interest in mind and trust that His plan for the two of us was ideal. Once I accepted that truth, I could start trusting Him. But trusting God does not guarantee we will always get what we want, which was not something I wanted to consider.

While still learning to surrender my will to God and trust His way, I had a preferred plan of how things would be with Jenna if she returned from out of town single and if God allowed. I would let her parents know that I wanted to court their daughter and ask Jenna's dad for her hand. I knew the exact ring she wanted and planned to get it, then put together a brilliant proposal. I was going to fix all the broken areas in my life myself so that I would be ready for this kind of commitment, but God had a better plan. And I needed to get to the point in my life where I would not only accept that but prefer it. There have been times in my life when I have asked God for something I wanted and didn't get it. Then, I later realized that if God had given me what I wanted at the time, it would have been bad for me. My life turned out better because God did not give me those things. It is comforting to know that God knows best and has my best interest in mind.

CHAPTER 8: TRUST

As I grew to desire what God wanted for me more than what I wanted for myself, I gained more peace of mind. That peace depended on my willingness to trust God's will or plan as better than mine, even if I didn't understand it. When I found it hard to trust God, it was because I feared trusting Him might not get me what I preferred, revealing my lack of trust. I had gotten my way before, and when it all played out, I was not satisfied with what I got. Getting my way was not in my best interest.

You can't say that no one has ever hurt or disappointed you; otherwise, you probably wouldn't be reading this book. Being in a relationship necessitates a willingness to go through both hurt and disappointment. Still, I tried to find a way to build trust rather than give up without expecting anyone except God to never disappoint me. My preferred expectations were the source of my disappointment, not God. God never disappoints. I felt disappointed because God was not doing what I wanted, but that disappointment was because I had wrong expectations. Instead of trusting God and wanting His best, I wanted what I preferred. I should have known that even though I can't always trust others, I can always trust God.

Trusting God means I will have some unanswered questions, yet I will trust Him anyway. That meant not needing the reason why God wanted me to bless Jenna's sister. It also meant not needing to know when or how the eventual outcome or purpose behind the never-ending Jenna drama would unfold. I did not understand why God had me carrying box after box up and down stairs, loading my car one trip after another. Thinking selfishly, it's not always fun going out of your way day after day for someone who does not know what you did for their family member. But as a doer of good who trusts in God, I did enjoy helping and getting to know Whitney's side of the family and imagining being an uncle to two more children and having a sister-in-law. I never knew if Jenna was privy to me helping her sister, nor did we ever discuss it. They infrequently spoke at the time, so I assumed my goodwill labor would go on anonymously. So, I trusted that God had a plan and that it was better than mine.

Part of trusting God meant I didn't stop trusting Him when I had a question with no answer. Although I did not know the answer, I could rest assured that God did. When I trusted God, I experienced peace. But when I didn't trust Him, I experienced fear and worry, which left me with two choices: I could trust God's plan and purpose or not. So I asked God to help me trust Him and acknowledged that He knew best.

God's in Control

I was always trying to figure things out, wanting to be in control of my life. But the world presents us with an endless array of problems; as soon as you conquer one, another challenge arises. One day, I paid to replace a couple of broken appliances; the water heater burst and needed replacing. Not long after that, the roof needed repair. The relief I experienced at one moment was brief. In the old days, I would have sought to understand some logical reason for all this. Now I trust that God has a purpose, and I don't need all the answers. He's someone I can trust with control in the "411" as well as the "911" times of life. Give me a broken appliance any day; a broken heart requires more trust. Through that experience, I have learned that there is only one relationship where I will never have my heart broken. It is my relationship with Jesus. Others may hurt me, but He will not. He is my comforter.

Trusting Through Pain

Moving all those boxes and household items up and down stairs from one home to the next day after day brought pain. It brought joy to my spirit helping Jenna's sister, but I bumped my head and hurt my knee. I also changed or rearranged my schedule so much that it was humorous. But all those little issues were preparation for God to bring me to trusting Him through a new level of pain—and this kind of pain would be much more severe.

After discovering Jenna's betrayal later that year on Thanksgiving at her sister's home, that pain was a broken heart. But it is better to trust with a chance of getting hurt than to quarantine your heart. If you have experienced hurt as I have, God is waiting to heal you: "He heals the brokenhearted and binds up their wounds" (Psalm 147:3, NIV). He will build a wall of protection around you.

God had important things for me to do and people to help, so I needed to get well. I needed to recover from the one who had frozen me in the pain of the past. It did not happen overnight. It developed little by little as I continued to trust God.

Proverbs compares a self-reliant individual to a fool. God wanted my reliance to be on Him, not myself. I told God, "I can't take this anymore," but that only meant that I was trying to do what God did not design me to do. I was trying to carry a load not intended for me. I needed to release that weight to the Lord: "Cast all your anxiety upon him because he cares for you" (1 Peter 5:7, NIV). Trusting God was another step in my healing process.

Trusting While Waiting

Trust helped me to enjoy life rather than survive it. Trusting God did not mean I could sit around doing nothing, waiting for God to do it all for me. Instead, I was doing what I could while leaving what I could not do to God. I had to do whatever God would lead me to do through the Holy Spirit in prayer, through the Bible, and through the people whom God put in my life. "When the Spirit of truth comes, he will guide you into all truth... He will tell you about the future" (John 16:13, NLT).

Depending on the Lord took the pressure off me as I trusted Him while letting the Holy Spirit lead my heart in a specific direction.

Times of doing nothing and letting God do for me did not mean I was inactive. While trusting God to take care of my problem, I engaged in prayer. In these prayers, rather than making more requests, I thanked God that He is in control. This confidence in God built trust. While waiting, whatever changes life threw my way, I trusted in the one who never changes.

Trusting's Final Thoughts

I learned a lot from helping Jenna's sister. It taught me that God would find a way to bless me if I trusted Him and did good. I discovered that trust requires not knowing God's plan and that His plan is better than mine. He's not asking me to figure it out; He's asking me to believe that He already has. To help me believe, God gives me things I can't handle so I will learn to rely on Him to handle them. I had a hard time trusting God until I knew that He will always make the wrong things in my life right in the end. I just needed to trust that He will do this in His way and timing.

I've learned that suffering doesn't destroy faith; it refines it. And God is worth trusting, even when you can't see the road ahead. Trust increased my confidence in God and removed the stress, worry, and fear that things between Jenna and I would fail. Trust brought peace of mind as I knew God had my best interests in mind. Trusting God was part of my healing process. It may be hard to understand why a broken heart can hurt worse than physical pain, but trusting God allowed me to enjoy life rather than push through it. Bottom-line is, trusting God combined with doing good solved many of my problems.

> "Trust in the Lord with all your heart and do not lean on your own understanding. In all your ways acknowledge Him, and He will make your paths straight" (Proverbs 3:5–6, NASB).

CHAPTER 9: FORGIVENESS

"Be kind to one another, tender-hearted, forgiving each other, just as God in Christ also has forgiven you" (Ephesians 4:32, NASB1995).

*I*t was a calm June night after our shift at work that still lingers in the hall closet of my mind. After a night of working together for Makara, Jenna, still unaware that I had been and continued to work for free, helped her make drinks and serve while she charmed the testosterone-drooling male customers drawn by her aura. I had a more modest yet definite following of female patrons, some of whom I had to ward off intoxicated advances physically, but nothing like Jenna, and none I had eyes for more than my Cover Girl. As we walked side-by-side to her car, Jenna said it at last—drawing attention to herself in a way a red circle on a math test shows you where you went wrong.

"Sorry," she blurted out in a soft, poignant voice while crossing the street.

I understood, even though she did not elaborate. It would be the only moment of apology I would receive in person for the year-long nightmare she had no idea I had endured. Little did she realize I had already forgiven her long ago, at great cost, for my sanity and own peace of mind. I acquired that ability to forgive through long suffering and yielding to God for help day by day—an invaluable lesson. The only problem was it went on week after week for month after month. It took listening to Pastor Colin S. Smith's sermon on forgiveness over a hundred times as a reminder to forgive. Listening while driving, I played the CD every weekend on my way to work for Makara. I had to cultivate the momentum necessary to carry me past the bitterness and resentment. The brokenness that only God can heal and remove from our hearts took the longest to eradicate.

Forgiveness is a process, not an event. It takes time to work through the emotional healing. There was a text from Jenna that summer of 2018 that summed it up:

"I'm sorry for what I have put you through. Truly. I love and care for you tremendously, and the last thing I've ever wanted to do was hurt you or our friendship. You are so special, and you always have been. I have always felt this way. I think we should sit down and talk."

It would be six weeks before she would bring it up one last time in person while working together for Makara.

"When I'm mentally ready, I want to spend the day together outside of work to talk," she said with a serious face.

"Okay" was my accepting response without asking her to expound.

We did sit down together one night after work at a nearby restaurant for some private one-on-one time over a shared meal like old times. But that day of talking about it never came, not even by the publishing of this book six years later. Our cozy dinner that evening was more about her realizing the forgiveness was genuine, for I never brought up the elephant in the room. I knew more heart-wrenching details of the betrayal than she realized, yet I did not hold her accountable for an explanation. By God's grace, I had released all my perturbed bitterness and anger in the name of Jesus. What this meant for our future remained unseen, but my silent feelings for her never swayed from unwavering loyalty. So, journey with me down the road of forgiveness.

Forgiving Isn't Easy

Forgiveness is hard and painful. Jenna realized she had wronged me, but she had no idea how much she had hurt me. "Human nature in action is wrongdoers blaming everybody but themselves. We are all like that," according to Dale Carnegie. Still, I forgave her. The alternative is of no gain—losing my closest friend (or trying to regain that) would not have been worth it: "Love prospers when a fault is forgiven, but dwelling on it separates close friends" (Proverbs 17:9, NLT). Now, don't confuse forgiveness with weakness. It called for significant strength of character and required confidence to offer and maintain true forgiveness, which came from deep within. I had to let go of the offense. It took solid fortitude and dependence upon the Lord to maintain that forgiveness and it was harder than she realized. But regardless of how hard it was, I forgave anyway. It played a vital role in the healing of my broken heart.

Most people want to forgive, but it took me a while to get there. Even when I did, it took extra reaffirmations of full forgiveness. Someone had done me a great wrong. At first, forgiving her seemed impossible. It felt debilitating, like a mountain I couldn't climb. It took mercy and unconditional love when that request for forgiveness took a long time in coming. It took time. It was like building up momentum to jump a hurdle rather than starting from standing still. How was I going to get over the difficult hurdle of the wrong done to me?

It took being kind, tenderhearted, and forgiving, as it says in Ephesians 4. I couldn't dwell on the offense. Whenever I thought about how wrong it all was, it only stirred up a fire within me. Bitterness and anger are fires that need fuel to remain in our thoughts, so I had to stop feeding them. Releasing bitterness was even more crucial while I awaited repentance. Jenna knew she had done a great wrong to me but was unaware of the severity of what she caused me to go through. She will never know or understand the suffering I experienced or the strength it took to forgive her. It took compassion to forgive her for the transgression she was too blind to see. While struggling to forgive, I had to think of all that God has forgiven me through Jesus Christ. I forgave because God has forgiven me much more.

Forgiveness Is Chosen

Holding on to anger and bitterness from the pain would have hindered my prayers and trust in God. "Forgiveness is a choice that you make and not a feeling that you have," according to Pastor Chip Ingram. I listened to him preach on the subject one Sunday in church: "Anger is not the problem—it is the warning light," he said. Anger was like a red light on my car dashboard, indicating a problem under the hood. Feeling anger is a natural reaction to betrayal, but choosing to forgive rather than remain angry is a choice I had to make.

Overcoming that anger was key to forgiveness. The Bible is clear that I was to forgive Jenna even before going to God in prayer: "And when you stand praying, if you are holding anything against anyone, forgive them…" (Mark 11:25, NIV). If I expected God to work in my life while I refused to forgive her, I was mistaken. Holding on to unforgiveness would only hurt me more. It is like drinking poison while thinking it is going to hurt the other person. It does not work that way. It would have eaten away at me from the inside out, making things worse in the end.

I had to consider the example Jesus displayed on the cross when it comes to forgiveness. Jesus spent approximately six hours of suffering on the cross for me. He only spent a couple of minutes of that time speaking. Some of the few words He spoke while hanging in pain exhibit what forgiveness looks like: "Father, forgive them for they know not what they are doing" (Luke 23:34, NIV). Like Jesus, I chose forgiveness.

Forgiveness Isn't Confrontational

Every secular book I read, video I watched, or podcast I listened to suggested forgiveness. But they all also urged confrontation with the offender or betrayer of trust. I'll never forget when Jenna first returned from her wayward ways and walked into work to greet me behind the bar, having been informed by Makara prior that I had been covering her shifts in her absence. She unabashedly acted as if nothing had happened the past eight months, as if there were no skip in the beat of our relationship. It was a bold move on her part made more manageable by others being around us while working for Makara when the encounter occurred. This brazen assurance did not surprise me much, given that Jenna could walk into a party like she was walking into a Carly Simon song. She approached me behind the counter in adroit excitement, sticking her phone in my face to show me something she had been doing. All whimsy smiles, she leaned into my left shoulder with a ballerina's smoothness, the comfort of a teddy bear, and the slickness of a used car salesman.

CHAPTER 9: FORGIVENESS

"Michael! You have to see this video interview for my new line of designs!" exclaimed Jenna with enthusiasm in her tone, a sugar-coated smile on her face, and an eyebrow raised.

Flipping her hair and grinning ear to ear, she waited for a reaction like a spokesmodel showing off a dinette set on *The Price Is Right*. It was at this ingenious moment when I had the choice to confront her or exercise forgiveness. Despite the supposed importance of confrontation, and even though I knew what she was doing, I played along. Besides, her incredible acting skills and nerve left me tongue-tied in awe. I watched her video interview and models wearing her designs, allowing Jenna to regain her comfort level while pressing up against me like old times. I said nothing (most women I've met are more verbal and the men more visual), but I did not look for any opportunity to confront, condemn, criticize, or complain. (I knew this was an attempt to deflect the real reason she went to LA and instill the thought it had everything to do with starting her fashion line). Instead, I continued to forgive with kindness before she ever expressed regret—things I learned from Dale Carnegie and the Bible. I had the right to confront, according to all the naysayers of selflessness and supporters of conditional pardon. The future may hold the need for confrontation, but only forgiveness and mercy were on the menu that day.

The Forgiveness Gesture

When Jenna returned from her extended absence and found forgiveness waiting that warm Friday evening, she came prepared with her own good tidings just in case her charm was insufficient to earn clemency.

"I have your birthday gift in my car that I brought back from LA for you, Michael," she stated proudly, standing erect. "It's been in my car traveling with me for months," she added.

I smiled, masking my bewilderment. I didn't know how to respond in words at that moment without some drivel. And I lacked the temerity to ask questions about how this came to be. All she did was flirt a little with me that night, and I drank it up like a mule at an oasis. Though my heart leaped for joy after realizing she had been thinking about me during her absence, a puzzling thought popped into my head: *My birthday was ten months ago. What took so long if that present was juggling around in your car the whole time?*

This present wasn't something she could have acquired that long ago when that other guy was in the picture. How would she have explained that to him unless he was unaware? That gift probably carried some weight, given that it was a constant reminder of imminent possible confrontation and rejection. It must have been an appeasement offering, like extending a handshake of agreement or hug after confirmation of forgiveness. My acceptance of this gesture was confirmation to her that my forgiveness was genuine. Later that evening, after walking Jenna to her car at the end of our shift, she opened the back door and presented me with her peace offering.

"Here you go. Maybe you can sing a song for me one day with it?" she asked with her arms extended, head tilted a little, and chin down as if to communicate, "Ah, please? I've asked this before."

"Thank you" was all I could say. Jenna knew I collected electric guitars. This shiny black six-string Squier would find a proper place of distinction on my living room wall. Though a kiss and warm embrace followed by a "forgive me" plea would have been my preference, this was the next best thing. My thank-you hug was a vindication that forgiveness was as real as the gift.

The Job Story

God had plans for me through my suffering. He was preparing me for the person I had been praying to forgive. Someone dearest to me had done me wrong in the most unforgivable way possible, requiring me to pass the test of forgiveness. I wanted quick resolution and success, but God wanted to improve me before promoting me in His timing. That required me to let all bitterness and unforgiveness go so God could bless me. While learning about forgiving, I looked to the Bible for examples of forgiving through suffering and found the story of Job in the Old Testament.

Job prayed to forgive his friends, who judged and criticized him during his time of suffering. His trust in God and mercy through pain resulted in him receiving a double blessing. Exercising forgiveness led to God giving him double for his trouble: "After Job had prayed for his friends, the Lord restored his fortunes and gave him twice as much as he had before" (Job 42:10, NIV). Even Job's new children received a blessing, including his daughters: "Nowhere in all the land were there found women as beautiful as Job's daughters, and their father granted them an inheritance along with their brothers" (Job 42:15, NIV). Stories like this made forgiveness without confrontation possible for me. It was comforting to know that whatever God takes away or requires me to give up, He will give me more than I had before if I trust Him and forgive my offenders.

Joseph's Forgiveness Story

The Genesis story of Joseph is one of forgiveness for unjust suffering. Joseph revealed to his brothers having dreams of them bowing before him. This boast stirred his brothers into a rage of jealousy. They threw him in a pit and then sold him into slavery to a traveling caravan of Ishmaelites, who took Joseph to Egypt and sold him to Potiphar, the captain of Pharaoh's guard.

Potiphar's wife also took notice of Joseph and tried to seduce him. But Joseph refused, so she falsely accused him. This charge landed him in prison, where he remained for several years. With God's help, Joseph correctly interpreted the dreams of two prisoners. One was Pharaoh's cupbearer, the other his baker. These dream interpretations eventually led to Joseph doing the same for Pharaoh, who put Joseph in charge of Egypt. When the brothers came to buy grain from Joseph during a famine, Joseph recognized them, but they did not know who he was, for it had been many years since they had seen him. The brothers all bowed to Joseph because he was an "important" person, just like Joseph had dreamed many years before. Joseph broke down in tears, revealing to his brothers, "I am Joseph, your brother, the one you sold, but do not be afraid."

Joseph suffered in prison for years because of his brothers, yet he forgave them without confrontation. It is no wonder God blessed him. Like Joseph, I have endured a long period of suffering due to the actions of another and still forgave. If you have not, I can assure you; you'll have the opportunity one day like me.

Jesus Forgave Most

No one forgave more than Jesus, so I try to follow His lead. One of the most famous and often quoted demonstrations of forgiveness is also in the Bible. In a show of His divinity, Jesus forgave a woman caught in the act of adultery. The spiritual leaders of the day brought her to Him and wanted to see if Jesus, claiming to be the Son of God, would follow the Law of God and have the woman stoned. Instead, Jesus welcomed the stoning, beginning with the first person who felt like he was without sin. In other words, this was a calling for a sinless person who did not deserve a stoning of their own. They all dropped their rocks and walked away. When Jesus looked up from drawing in the dirt, the woman was standing there alone, with no accusers. Asking her if there was anyone left to accuse her of her sin, she answered, "No." Jesus responded, "Neither do I condemn thee: go, and sin no more" (John 8:11, KJV). Forgiveness is an attribute of God I learned from reading the Bible so that I, too, can forgive others. This one story alone was reason enough to drop my stone when it came to forgiving Jenna.

Forgive Them All

I have had to exercise forgiveness in both business and my personal experiences to maintain peace of mind in my own life. I've given money without compensation or repayment. People have scammed me in business and investments for hundreds of thousands. Some have been rude in their treatment of me in exchange for the kindness I have shown them. I've experienced betrayal from someone I loved. And yet I forgave them all. "A lifetime's not too long to live as friends," according to iconic Christian musician Michael W. Smith. I couldn't be a friend for a lifetime with unforgiveness in my soul.

Through my forgiving experience with Jenna, I learned that the way you behave toward someone who has wronged you speaks volumes about you to them. How I treated her was much more important than the discomfort I felt from how she had treated me. Have you ever forgiven someone who never apologized? I never knew how strong I was until I had to forgive someone who wasn't sorry and accept an apology I never really received.

I could not hold onto my unforgiveness. I had to let it go and give it to the God of justice, who always makes wrong things right (see Isaiah 30:18). If I were willing to do things God's way, He would make it up to me. So as Joseph, Job, and Jesus did, I forgave Jenna for the hurt and betrayal she never realized I endured.

Final Forgiving Thoughts

For me, forgiveness was a process, not an event. It took time, and it wasn't easy. For my love story to prosper, I had to forgive. Dwelling on it would only separate close friends. Forgiveness was painful, and it took me a while to get there. It felt like a mountain I couldn't climb. It required mercy and unconditional love when that request for forgiveness never came. But there was never a choice in my mind, for it is through Jesus Christ I owe an enormous debt, and God who has forgiven me much more.

> "Bear with each other and forgive one another if any of you has a grievance against someone. Forgive as the Lord forgave you" (Colossians 3:13, NIV).

CHAPTER 10: GIVING

"Now this I say, he who sows sparingly will also reap sparingly, and he who sows bountifully will also reap bountifully. Each one must do just as he has purposed in his heart, not grudgingly or under compulsion, for God loves a cheerful giver" (2 Corinthians 9:6–7, NASB1995).

Andrew (not his real name) is a friend of mine. That twenty-dollar bill I slipped into his hand the first day we met a couple of years earlier sealed our friendship. Andrew used to do landscaping for a living, but he developed diabetes. It led to him having open-heart surgery and his legs cut off below the knees. His girlfriend sometimes pushes him around in his wheelchair, but it is typical to see him alone. She lives with him in his apartment behind the grocery store where I shop.

Usually, I see him sitting in his wheelchair near the entrance a few times each week. We chat for as long as I can without intruding on his solicitation for the donations of others. On a typical day, I take him his beverage of choice, a snack, or the meal he requests. If I miss him on the way in, he lets me know it with a "Hey!" Sometimes, he yells for me to get him this or that on my way into the store. But he often motions for me to come over and take his order. Most of the time, he says, "Thank you" or "God bless" when I return with his request, but not always. Andrew does not know my name. He knows nothing about me and has never asked. If Andrew wants something that requires more cash than I brought for myself, I try not to complain. So why do I do this? I do it because I do it unto the Lord—period. There are few things more important than giving at the expense of something you want. Doing so amid your brokenness adds an even more abundant blessing. The Lord sees all our secret sacrificial giving. He rewards in this life and the life to come. So let's dive into my giving story.

Giving Makara Time

When I started working for Makara, she needed time and money. Only weeks after learning of Jenna's betrayal via social media, I was working for free for Makara to save Jenna's job. More important to Makara was that $1,000 in cash I gave her as a Christmas gift to help her business that month. Of course, she refused the cash-filled envelope at first. I had already started working for free and given her the tips each night. How could she accept more? But I insisted, and it was a good thing I did. Within a few weeks, she needed $11,000 more as a short-term loan, not a gift—she insisted this time at her request.

I'd set aside those funds for my property taxes. Months passed, and I still did not know when or if I would ever see that money again. I then had to pay those taxes from other resources as an unanticipated expense. Two years later, my short-term loan ended with payment back and a smile of relief from Makara. By then, I had already considered it a gift, so when she repaid the $11,000, it was an unexpected blessing to us both. It gave Makara time to run her business for two more years and led to many stories involving Jenna. But while that cash kept Makara's business open, the doing mattered most. Giving her my time was far more valuable than just giving her money.

Giving Jenna Credit

Jenna and I celebrated her birthday over Thai food in San Francisco, but the real reason for the destination was a well-known department store for a designer belt she had her heart set on getting. Given that tiny waistline, the object of her desire was not available in her size. Though I offered to appease her with anything else she might want, she had one thing in mind. So she needed a pick-me-up for her wish to come true. Given her skill in finding what she wanted, she found the place with her size. Since she would be traveling there the following week, it seemed the appropriate gifting opportunity. Still down over not getting what she wanted on her actual birthday, we were working for Makara together when I gave her the good news two nights later.

"Here. Take this with you when you travel to Canada next week, and get your belt there and whatever else you need," I said with a smile.

Grabbing hold of my Visa, she smiled back with those pearly whites.

"Yes! Thank you, Michael. That is so sweet of you," she exclaimed with one of her exuberant hugs. You know the kind—the joyful ones that almost knock you over. I have to give the girl some credit. She loves shopping opportunities, and I enjoyed giving them to her.

Giving Jenna Props

Jenna was a bit of an actress, so her area of expertise wasn't exactly giving. It was believing she was awesome and working hard to charm people into thinking so, too—as I did. When we'd get together or work the same shift, she'd use my name in conversation frequently, a successful technique used to hypnotize whipped givers like me who like the sound of their names coming from their crush. And it worked.

"I'll come over, then let's go get Tai food, Michael."

Duh, okay.

"Wanna share my steak with me on our break, Michael?"

Double dumb, dumb would be a response of anything other than "YES."

I've met girls who are so self-centered and don't like sharing anything, let alone giving, including clothes, money, attention, and food. They remind me of Daffy Duck's "mine, mine, mine, all mine" policy. Jenna was a giver at heart, if not always in practice. She had what it takes in street smarts, wit, and good looks to rise to the top, like cream on the dessert of her choice. And we had delirious fun together over inside jokes, silly dreams, and shared goals. She was tender and sweet with children and animals.

What I delighted in—the humor inherent in quipping little things so dumb they were good, or at least funny—like how she would baby talk with made-up words to babies or puppies. But Jenna didn't kowtow to anyone to curry favor other than her parents or an infant to get a smile. And when we worked together during a rush, I was Captain Intensity, fundamentally incompatible with someone as laid back yet spontaneous as Jenna. But I am unabashed to give her props for balancing me out and making me fancy the relative importance of things like the joy of hearing your name pronounced endearingly by your muse.

Giving Jenna Blessings

It was Friday, November 30, 11:30 p.m., and Jenna was following me home. We had both finished working early for Makara, who had asked Jenna if she had stayed in my guestroom recently. Knowing I had prepared a surprise for Jenna over the past few weeks, Makara's curiosity started piquing. Curious herself at that point, the early ending of our shift provided Jenna with the chance. Heading up the staircase like she owned the place, Jenna had no idea of what was to come. I followed, secretly recording the drama about to unfold on my hidden cellphone. Opening the door, she flicked on the light switch, which lit up the guestroom with a couple hundred bulbs' blinding brightness.

"Oh my God!" she exclaimed. "What the heck?" She giggled as she dropped her purse to the floor in shock. "This is the most gorgeous room I've ever been in. It's like the room of my dreams!" Jenna emphasized with her mouth open and jaw dropped. "When did you do this?" she asked.

But before I could answer, she blurted out again, "Oh my God! What? I don't know how to… Oh, that's so cute," she said, looking at one of the many items to catch her eye. "I don't know what to say. I'm, like, speechless, and it's all so gorgeous! Aw. This room is the most beautiful room I've ever seen," she repeated with a big smile. "Why does it smell so beautiful?"

"If it's too strong, I can…" was all I could utter before she cut me off.

"No, no, no. I love it, Michael!" she insisted. "No one has ever done something like this for me before," she admitted. "This is the most beautiful room! I am obsessed with it. Okay, I think we should FaceTime Makara! Can I show her?" she asked, smiling as she gazed around the room in wonder.

Tiny, soft white lights surrounded a mirror within a white horizontal door nailed above the headboard. More of the little lights encircled the new white vanity and mirrors to one side of the bed. Atop the vanity lay professional lipsticks, blush, cotton balls, beauty supplies, a glass perfume jar, and a crystal cross. Long pearls wrapped around the vanity mirror, and the vanity drawer opened up to MAC makeup brushes and more beauty items. The vanity wall, plastered with Jenna's magazine covers and surrounded by lights, was jaw-dropping. With her initials imprinted on the wall, on candles, and on wood, it was a woman's ultimate home away from home. The two end tables, filled with little things she liked, left space for new clothes.

A heart-shaped designer glass vase filled with lights topped one end table. The other, an antique from Paris, displayed her Bible and devotionals under the glass top. Two ends of the room each had designer Paris mannequins dressed in jewelry facing one another. Unique mason jars filled with soft little lights decorated the floor. Soft mink rugs surrounded the bed, covered with white bedding and matching pillows. A jeweled princess stool draped with a white, silky-soft, furry comforter added a touch of majesty. New clothes I had bought her when shopping together hung in the closet with tags still attached. Below was her own custom white laundry basket. The guest bathroom, decorated with white towels and all the necessary female supplies, lay in wait. A white marble cup and matching toothbrush holder encircled the sink. It was everything a princess would need.

Jenna now had her very own private custom guestroom and bathroom in my home to go along with the key I had given her long ago. Not only had she experienced forgiveness but now over-the-top generosity. There are few more peaceful sensations than giving an unexpected blessing. Don't misunderstand. I was not a starry-eyed wimp, letting Jenna walk all over my generous nature. I was exercising mercy and proving my forgiveness genuine through giving. Besides, the room was in my home, which meant others could use it should Jenna return to her wayward ways.

Giving Jenna Sight

It was Christmas season that same year, and Jenna had concluded that her vision was weaker in one eye. It was not long before we were off to rectify the problem at the mall for glasses shopping. These were not sunglasses that we set sail for—they were prescription eyewear. Spending too much time on that little device she holds dear and near to her face had led to this. After I paid for the doctor's exam, it came time to select frames.

The story could end there, but no, this was Jenna, and she likes style and fashion. Those Tiffany frames were not the most expensive the store had to offer, but they were close and worth it to her. And why not Tiffany? I'd been to that store of little 1837 blue (but is more of a seafoam green) colored boxes for her before. My computer glasses were half the cost of hers on my last visit, and I needed new ones soon as well, but again, this was Jenna, and she came first. Once again, this became a gift that brought more smiles and giggles. Love wants the other person to be happy, and you'll sacrifice if necessary to make that happen. Others always come first when it comes to sacrificial giving, and few things offer more of a blessing.

Giving Jenna Esteem

Jenna aspired to be an actress, a well-known published model, a pin-up, and a Cover Girl. She wanted to be a writer, fashion designer, successful businesswoman, and attorney. It was obvious she wanted to be a person of importance. She desired many things beyond material possessions, and I wanted to make them happen for her if possible.

Dr. John Dewey, one of America's most profound philosophers of the early twentieth century, said that the deepest urge in human nature is "the desire to be important." I imagined Jenna was a precocious child with a high IQ and a desire to succeed, so giving her a feeling of importance is exactly what I did. I asked her questions she enjoyed answering—about herself and listened with attentive ears while looking her in the eyes when she spoke, validating her opinions, supporting her beliefs, and calming her fears with sympathetic reassurance. I published her writing in my magazine. I published her pictures inside and on the covers of magazines and calendars. When she wanted pictures of her designs, I photographed them for her. And I supported all her hopes and dreams by becoming genuinely interested in them with all the admiration and recognition I could muster. Our history was replete with the sheer witchery (in a good way) of me giving her praise. I gave her the recognition and place of importance she wanted, and it blessed both of our lives in the process. It was a joy living to give her esteem.

Happiness Follows Giving

Winston Churchill once said, "You make a living by what you earn and a life by what you give." I have lived that. Before I started giving, my life was missing something. When life is only about your next meal, business deal, payday, or vacation, it's not very satisfying. Money can buy things, but it can't buy peace of mind. Happiness doesn't come from buying the latest stuff but rather from giving. When I gave to others, I also experienced some relief from my brokenness. It brought healing to my soul and body as well. When I would give to others, it made life more rewarding. It was hard at first, but in time, I looked at life differently being a giver. Living generous, like I was with Jenna's designer belt, glasses, and room, never made me miss the self-centered life I once led. It also trickled over to all areas of my life lest I ever foolishly think God's idea of giving meant only meeting every whim of Jenna while neglecting other, more worthwhile causes.

Living as a generous giver sounded unrealistic at first, but as a broken person, I grabbed for relief any way I could. Opportunities don't have to fall off the shelf into my lap like me noticing Andrew every day. All that is necessary is looking for an opportunity to give. There are lots of other broken people out there in need. Doing something generous about it without telling anyone made me want to do it again.

I have a friend who owns a restaurant. She's always giving homeless people a free meal or money, and hardly anyone knows this. When you feed the hungry, poor, and weak, you are feeding the Lord (see Matthew 25:35–40). She's always there to listen and help broken people with their problems. Her reward is a great sense of joy that comes from helping those who can't return the favor. And when you are hurting, you are better off helping someone else. Reaching out and helping hurting people helped me forget my pain from betrayal, especially when assisting the one who caused it.

Giving and Receiving

Giving is receiving in disguise, so I give and receive. I enjoy being a giver like my friend. The Bible says, "Ask, and you will receive" (Matthew 7:7, CEV). Well, when you give, sometimes there is a fine line between giving and receiving. What you get back can be better than what you offer. Jesus Himself said, "It is more blessed to give than receive" (Acts 20:35, NIV). I can testify to the truth of this verse. I'm always the last one to open Christmas presents. The reason is simple—it is more enjoyable for me to view others opening the gifts I gave them.

Here's a statement that may not sound logical, but it was true for me: sometimes, our emotional need to give may exceed the other person's need to receive. Spending money on myself never improved my happiness much, but spending money on others did. It is rare for me to go to the mall and buy something for myself. I would much rather shop for someone else, and I don't mean only for Jenna. The joy that comes from the surprise they receive is priceless. And the amount spent is not a factor. The simple act of spending money on someone else would lift my spirits, and when it came at a sacrifice, even more so. But how much I spent on others did not matter as much as the fact that I did it.

There are two types of people in the world: givers and takers. The takers may eat better, but the givers sleep better. Life isn't about me; it's about discovering who God created me to be. God created me to be a giver, not a taker. Giving makes me feel as if my life has more meaning. It makes me feel as if there is a real purpose to my life and that others need me. No matter how many magazines, covers, or editorial pages published my work, it's giving my life away to others that has made me happy. Giving, even in small ways, has health benefits too. It can help you live longer as the joy it brings will strengthen your immune system: "A joyful heart is good medicine, but a broken spirit dries up the bones" (Proverbs 17:22, NASB). So I give to be happier and healthier.

Giving with Wisdom

Giving does not go to waste, but I try to be wise in my giving. "Sometimes the gift that makes the least sense brings the most joy," says Brad Formsma, author of *I Like Giving*. I find it hard to trust people on the street who beg for money, but I do not let abusers of my kindness discourage me. I once bought Andrew the meal he requested and sat in my car for a few minutes out of sight. To my surprise, he blithely stored it behind his wheelchair and returned to begging. What did I learn from that? Not much. "You don't have to know the extent of someone's need, so don't take personal offense to a perceived deception," says Brad. Still, I liked Andrew regardless of that observation because he was not blandishing but had a real need, unlike the cajole mountebank men some women I know have described to me.

People like my friend benefit more from ongoing help than a one-time gift anyway. Even so, if I feel led, I give something. If I give cash, I hope they don't waste it. This concept was hard for me to swallow at one time, but when I give now, it doesn't mean I have to know that the money is going to good use. When I provide for others with a good heart, it releases the recipient to do what they want with my gift. The fact that I care means more than what I give.

If you'd asked me years ago what my life is all about, I may have said something about being successful in my photography business. That's not so much my thinking anymore. Being a little wiser now, I live to give and always look for an excuse to give my clients more than they expect. Jesus said that it is better to give than receive, and

I now know that's true. Trying to prove myself a success, in the end, isn't going to matter. I won't ask myself on my deathbed how much is in my bank account. I'll care more about the relationships I formed, some of which grew from giving.

Giving is a privilege, and God has blessed me with the resources and wisdom to do so. It is something I get to do rather than something I have to do. It brings me joy, for all my gifts have resulted in a smile rather than a frown. There are so many broken people in this world, but I can't fix them all. It's my pleasure to help those I can.

Giving Creates Excitement

Giving made my life more exciting, which was encouraging when I was falling apart inside. I may have been hurting, but there are a whole lot of other hurting people out there as well. I just needed to open my eyes to notice.

I probably worked with thousands of five-to-thirteen-year-old children as a part-time recreation leader for my city all through college and grad school. I taught them cooking, woodworking, archery, and bowling for seven years. I coached and refereed their football, t-ball, and basketball games. Giving my time, knowledge, and ability brought enjoyment to their lives and created as much excitement for me as it did for them. Seeing them grow, learn, improve, and develop skills they never expected was thrilling for me. I'll always remember how exciting it was to hand out awards to children who excelled at the end of each season. That giving experience shaped my entire life, made me the giving person I am today and proved to me that giving creates excitement. I now encourage others to give, especially when they are hurting. I never realized before how valuable it would be when brokenness surrounded me.

CHAPTER 10: GIVING

I used to have no problem buying myself things, but that's not very satisfying. What matters are things like Jenna's delightful reaction to her guestroom gift. It was such a joyous feeling to see her response to what I had done to give her that exciting experience. The problem with buying things for ourselves is those things fade with time, but giving stays in your heart forever. "For where your treasure is, there your heart will be also" (Matthew 6:21, NASB).

I learned that giving also involves more than things or money. Many women over the years have told me that I am a good listener. That skill developed through countless hours of waiting for makeup artists to finish working on models. My listening ear or the giving of my time became my gift. Many women I have met didn't always need money or advice. Now, don't get me wrong, most of them did, but plenty of them only needed someone to listen to them. And it made life exciting listening to their stories, dreams, and aspirations.

Two days ago, as I wrote this story, Jenna reminded me of her two favorite gifts she had ever received from me. I'll never forget how meaningful her words were to me.

"The portfolio with all my magazine covers!" she blurted out with excitement and a smile.

One present required a lot of time, effort, and money; the other needed some careful thought. Guess which one she mentioned first. You guessed right: the one that required more thought. You always know if someone loves you because they will look for some way to give to you. Becoming generous made me notice opportunities to pour love on others by giving. Those giving experiences made life more exciting and meaningful.

Giving and Getting

When I focused on what I lacked and wanted to obtain, I remained stuck in my brokenness. But when I focused on what God has given me and what I can give to others, I ended up getting so much more than I gave. Providing for others in need has bred good relationships for me.

I unstintingly worked free of charge for Makara for twenty-plus hours a week for two years. I even gave her all my tips when Jenna was not there. That giving experience cost me time and thousands of dollars per month. All the extra driving wore out my car until it broke down, leaving me without one. But our friendship grew, and the rewards from God were many. It gave me more opportunities to provide a loving, listening ear while serving hundreds of her customers well. Donating my time made me feel like I had more while giving away money made me feel wealthier. "When you invest your money into someone else's dream, you help yourself more than you help them. You strategically place yourself in a position to receive from God. What you make happen for others, God will make happen for you," says Teri Savelle Foy. I am living proof of that.

When I decided to give, I discovered resources I didn't know I had. I was a giver in one situation, but the blessing I got from giving made me feel like the recipient. The reason I thought this way is because giving and receiving are like two sides of the same coin: "Give generously to him, and do not let your heart be grieved when you do so. And because of this, the LORD your God will bless you in all your work and in everything to which you put your hand" (Deuteronomy 15:10, BSB). I am so grateful to Jesus for all he did for me. It is what initially converted me into being a giver. I don't give to get something back from God, trying to earn something, but it is comforting to know that He stands watch, blessing me for doing so anyway.

I was not in control of much with Jenna, but I could manage my giving. God never intended for our lives to be self-consuming, so I give mine away. "Give to everyone who asks of you, and whoever takes away what is yours, do not demand it back" (Luke 6:30, NASB). God did not create me so I could live for myself. When I focus on myself, life isn't that great. When generosity is a regular part of my day, however, life matters more. Others appreciate me, and I feel it. A sense of satisfaction comes from blessing others. As regular giving became part of my routine, life felt more meaningful. As a giver, I changed from asking how I could get ahead to how I could help. My giving experience brought more relief from my brokenness because giving is getting.

Giving and Loaning

I feel compelled to add one last personal story of warning about giving: being a giver rather than a lender, I love that giving is not loaning—and for a good reason. In my darkest moment, someone gave me a book to read at Christmas following the Thanksgiving confirmation of Jenna's betrayal. Receiving that unexpected gift was like a medic removing a dagger during a battle and then bandaging my wound with precision.

I anticipated the book would be of immense help and comfort, and that assumption was correct. It became a valued tool as I frequently reviewed the yellow highlighted words I had notated from its reading. I was so intrigued by its message that I bought the audio version of the book and listened to it repeatedly for the hope it gave. Because I had not asked for nor expected this gift, I overlooked a cold, self-centered side to this person for quite some time. I gave the person gifts in return now and then in appreciation. I did not expect gifts in return, nor did I receive any—the book was compensation enough. I once even did free photography and computer editing for this person upon their request when I would have charged a thousand dollars to anyone else.

Still grateful two and a half years after receiving the book, I found myself ordering another little surprise gift for this person online. The next day, I received a message from this person, who was not yet aware of my most recent gift. The message informed me that another individual was a good candidate for their book, so I could mail it back. It wasn't a request. It was a statement to send it back. At that moment, I realized my error in perceiving the heartfelt Christmas surprise was a gift rather than something on loan. That wrong assumption felt like someone tripped me, ripped off the bandage covering my chest, and stepped on my exposed wound with an army boot. For a moment, all the memories of the pain from Jenna's indiscretion flooded my mind with fear that it might return. This book was one you keep and study as a reference rather than reading once. I found it interesting that this person assumed I no longer needed or wanted the information.

I retreated to my room, dropped to my knees in prayer for God to forgive this person and me for any wrongdoing, then wept a little. I spent the next hour reviewing some of my yellow highlighted notes in the book one last time before mailing it back and never heard a peep about the book again or my markings in it. You may never know how much unintentional hurt you can inflict by loaning rather than giving when the accepted token is something perceived as a gift. It is one reason why I stopped lending money and things long ago. I only give things away now, putting into practice what I have learned from Luke 6:34–38.

Now, you might say, "What if someone asks to borrow my car, money, or something else that is significant that they truly need, and I'm able to do so?" If you do, prepare to pay what your insurance doesn't cover for any damage to your car and not expect or request a payment back for any cash loan. This concept may be hard to swallow, but it is one reason that motivated me to study money and giving in the Bible for years, in addition to reading several books on the subjects. I took away from that study that giving isn't lending, and a loan isn't a form of giving. I remember that every time someone wants to borrow something from me. Not being a lender of money or things anymore has saved me some unintended fuel to my brokenness. Being broken is one thing; being broke and broken is another. It is an unnecessary burden that would add to the problem I was trying to fix.

Final Giving Thoughts

I've seen opportunities to be generous everywhere. I haven't needed to make drastic life changes or start a nonprofit to become a giver. After this book's publication, I will ensure those who cannot afford it but need it get a copy. I plan to give any profits from sales to others in need and those who inspire me. That is how I will continue to give out of gratitude for all God has done for me.

I have friends who are a gift to others, as I was for Andrew and Jenna, but unaware of it. Rather than viewing their job as a way to make a living, they take pride in serving customers well as I did for Makara. They ask how they can serve or help others better or what it will take to meet a need. They know it's not necessary to be a millionaire to offer a gift or have a lot of money to be a productive giver. All that's needed is to start living the life of a giver.

Few things in this world feel as enjoyable as giving. Giving makes me more aware of the needs of others, and it makes life happy. Giving makes my life more meaningful and exciting. Jesus said it is better to give than receive, so I decided to be a giver rather than a loaner. Embracing generosity is now a habit of mine that has altered my life. My pain was screaming inside for so long. One day I will look back in amazement at how I have changed and how my brokenness departed.

On that day, I can say the greatest gift I've given anyone was an unspoken one. She will read these words before I ever get around to speaking them to her. Until then, a quote from my favorite Hallmark movie, *Once Upon a Christmas Miracle,* says it for me: "The greatest gift you can give anyone is love."

> "Give, and it will be given to you. A good measure, pressed down, shaken together and running over, will be poured into your lap. For with the measure you use, it will be measured to you" (Luke 6:38, NIV).

CHAPTER 11: SPOUSE

"He who finds a wife finds a good thing and obtains favor from the LORD" (Proverbs 18:22, BSB).

I cannot count the number of times I have quoted that passage as a part of my daily routine during the past four years. Kneeling beside my bed, the words from Proverbs 18:22 would come out as I said, "I want that kind of favor in my life, Lord." I've prayed this not because of some insecure need for a spouse but because I know what I want in one. "All the shine of a thousand spotlights, all the stars we steal from the night sky will never be enough. Towers of gold are still too little. These hands could hold the world, but it'll never be enough," according to Loren Allred, and I concur. Dust settles; I don't and won't. I want God's best, and I won't take her for granted! "Charm is deceptive and beauty is fleeting, but a woman who fears the LORD is to be praised" (Proverbs 31:30, BSB).

She's the One

I've only bought rings for two girls in my life. The first girl was a fourth-grader. I rode my bicycle two miles to pick out the tawdry pink gem at the five-and-dime store. In all honesty, I had an ulterior motive. It was her older sister whom I had an interest in pursuing through the shenanigan maneuver. Puppy love knows not what it is doing. That older sister was the most popular girl in school and by far the prettiest, so I pretended to be Mr. fancy-pants. She was out of my league in maturity and looked like she was in high school. Her full name is still embedded in my memory forever. Dana Lowrey. I'll never forget Dana pressing her soft lips against mine and slowly kissing me in sixth grade after class. It was my first kiss on the mouth, and she knew what she was doing. It's okay for you to break a smile here. The innocence of children is adorable.

The second ring I purchased was for Jenna over thirty years later. We were at Macy's shopping for her mother's Christmas present. It turned out to be another shopping spree for my sidekick as well. We did find a beautiful gift for her mom, but the sparkly, silver, swirling ring Jenna found for herself was the real reason for the season on this day.

"Oh, Michael, look! It's so beautiful, and with the discount, we can get this and my mom's gift," she begged with a sad face, tilted head, and giggle.

"Well then, I want a kiss in the car since we came here for your mom," was my regaled rebuttal with a grin.

"Yes!" with fluttering eyes was Jenna's response, the only one I hoped to hear.

I, of course, unapologetically caved. There was never a doubt. After all, Jenna had the ring glued to her finger the instant our saleswoman removed it from the display. Extending her arm and bending her wrist like a princess to view and show off her new showpiece in all its splendor was adorable. The dazzling ring did add a stunning, scintillating glow to her fragile yet beautiful hand as she gazed upon it. Watching her bounce up and down, heels to tiptoes, as the saleswoman rang up the sale was priceless. If she only knew how much I looked forward to one day shopping for her every week. It was not about giving her the world—it was about making her feel like she was the only one in it.

The three short thank-you kisses that later followed in the car were worth more than all the diamonds in Macy's. Her smile was more endearing than all the brides I had ever photographed combined. I paused and looked into her smiling eyes after the third kiss. If I had a superpower, it would be the ability to freeze time; that way, I could have made that moment last longer. I've never gotten engaged. I never even asked someone to marry me. A girl once told me that if I didn't marry her, I'd be walking her down the aisle one day for someone else. Six months later, I spoke at her wedding reception.

I've only made it clear to one woman that I wanted to marry her one day. We were at a friend's restaurant. She had already told me that she could see a future for us, but what came next confirmed it was no fluke.

"There are things about you that I just cannot replace with someone else," Jenna admitted in a soft, matter-of-fact way.

I was speechless for a moment—thrilled that she had come to this conclusion.

"I've also talked with my mom about you," was her follow-up.

"What did you tell her?" I asked with a smile in breathless curiosity, sleuthing for details.

"Only good things," she responded with a smirk.

It was a week later at that same restaurant, sitting at the bar with one hand on her leg, when I communicated my feelings. The date was September 2 of that year, fifteen months before the Christmas ring story above. It became a moment plastered in my mind.

"I want to be more than best friends and have been thinking beyond that," I boldly declared, looking into her eyes.

Jenna followed up with a description of the kind of ring she wanted. "3.5–4.0 carat princess cut diamond with a yellow gold band" was the precise description she gave.

No problem, I thought, not saying anything but only smiling in acknowledgment. I'd been waiting for this conversation since the fourth grade. I was in a state of la-la land, wanting this heart-fluttering sensation to never end, like when the first time someone tells you in school that your dreamboat has a crush on you. It was another moment when I would have used that superpower. We had our first kiss that night on a bench eating gelato; my performance wasn't my best work by far.

There was no long open-mouth action involved—at least not like I had learned from a pretty, well-developed blonde named Angie Ash in seventh grade. Being an eighth-grader, she pressed her cotton candy-tasting frosted, plump lips against my mouth, stuck her more experienced tongue down my unsuspecting throat, and taught me, a naïve twelve-year-old, how to French kiss for the first time while standing in her room one night. Wow. That was a mouthful. Given that Angie was out of my league in looks and more confident than my innocent mind, my stomach was doing summersaults. Still, I liked her aggressive tactics, though they were short-lived. I can still hear my mom honking the car horn from outside Angie's parent's home to pick me up way sooner than I would have preferred at that moment—cutting short my intro to crazy town sex education, less I digress.

Like junior high, I suppose I was about as nervous as that first time one gives a public speech before that first kiss with Jenna. After all, this was my best friend and wing-woman whom I was about to kiss for the first time, and we discussed the kiss before the showdown—adding to the pressure and intensity of the event.

"Are you nervous, Michael?" Jenna asked with a smirk. "Let's just do it," was her follow-up before I could la-di-da my way through a charming yet sensible-sounding response.

I think terrified and nervous would be the appropriate words to describe my feelings at that moment. So I hesitated, then moved in for one kiss, then another, slow but too brief for my preference, before a tiny bug landed on her gelato-glistened lower lip and stole the moment. Concern over my dull junior varsity mode of operation left me anxious and worried about messing up. And my southern-gentleman-like technique with Jenna would have been too prim and proper by eighth-grader Angie Ash's standards. I should have stopped worrying and waited more patiently on God's timing and leading. Ralph Waldo Emerson once wrote, "Adopt the pace of nature: her secret is patience." We would all do well to heed that advice.

I preferred for my relationship with Jenna to consist of snowflakes and butterflies. But in real life, we all know there are ups and downs in the romantic department; otherwise, I would not be writing about it. So I considered some questions about dating to find a spouse that I have pondered after years of talking with thousands of women.

What's the Vision?

I awoke out of bed one night, distinctly remembering another dream for the third time within twelve months. I was in a spacious, beautiful two-story house with vaulted ceilings, all bright white inside except for the large black sofa. A pretty woman with shoulder-length hair was sitting on the couch, wanting us to pick out a Disney children's movie to watch. What a beautiful sight.

I wanted to head straight for her but first had to hang up a shirt. Many other friendly people were in the house when I found myself downstairs by a coat rack. I was trying to put my shirt on the hanger when I noticed several other people's clothes on the coat rack. I preferred to join the woman on the sofa, but I went upstairs first and realized that nothing about this big house looked familiar. My room was small, with nothing on the white walls. There was one skinny bed to the left, thinner than a door, with a comforter; a white desk sat beside it. A lamp was the only thing on the desk, and another white desk was at the end of the bed. I asked a friend at the entrance to my room a logical question: "Why do I have the smallest room and the smallest bed, and why do I have two desks in my room?" I was mad and complaining, but I knew the Lord was calling me to lean into him like never before if I wanted His best. I took the frames off the skinny bed and put them on the other side of the room. Only a thin mattress and comforter remained. I then took the desk beside my bed and moved it to the end of the room with the other. Then my mom came to the door, so I asked her the same logical question with a twist: "Why must I have the skinniest bed in my room, and why do I have two desks when I own this house?" Then I woke up!

When I considered what I had envisioned, I sensed there was a spiritual lesson to glean from the many facets of this dream. I realized in my spirit and mind that the skinny bed represented my current suffering. The two desks symbolized God's calling for me. I was to study and seek Him twice as hard as I thought would be reasonable and fair for a Christian to espouse. When I contemplated the reason, I understood why. It was because I expected a double reward, a double recompense for all that I had gone through. And I figured my mom represented God because my mom was the one person who had unconditional love for me. So I shared this dream with my sister.

"What do you think the dream means?" I asked her in a curious voice. I was waiting for her to say if the woman was Jenna, but she didn't say either way.

"The woman wanting to watch the Disney movie with you was your future wife! And your home looked unfamiliar because it was your amazing new home the two of you would be living in together," she blurted out with confidence.

Wow! If that scenario were the result of the suffering part of the dream, it would all be worth it, much to the consternation of my sister. My future spouse is in God's hands. God doesn't think small, and He is not limited in His thinking, as we often are. So I trust God for big dreams and big rewards for my troubles, even if they do not seem realistic in the natural, like my future family home dream. God will never give me hope or an idea that matches my budget. He's not checking my bank account—He's testing my faith. The future belongs to those who believe in the beauty of their God-given dreams. If God gives me a dream or vision, I can do it. As I quoted before, I do so again: "What is impossible with man is possible with God" (Luke 18:27, NIV).

Who Is Directing?

I leave it in God's hands when it comes to finding "the one." If you are anything like me, you know what it is like to wait on the Lord's direction and guidance. When a man is walking according to his purpose, there is room for only one woman to walk with him. Still single, I try to be completely content with the Lord's will. His ideal spouse is not predetermined, but the best candidates will be much better than settling for what I may think is best. A woman of God is someone worth waiting patiently for. Nowadays, relationships last till whenever, but when God gets involved, they last forever. I want "the one," and at this point in my life, I don't want to date anyone that I wouldn't marry. I want her to know she fell in love with someone who looks at her like she's the only one in the room. That someone values everything about her. That someone will hold dear what others have overlooked. How do I know this? Because I have become that person for someone, and you know her name.

I could be the only male on Earth, and it would not make a difference. All the women in the world could have their sights set on me as their suitor, and it would not change anything. "The heart wants what it wants," according to Selena Gomez. I don't settle for less than God's best, and I'm not looking for something else. It's been that way for five years, and only the Lord can change that. Yes, I know what I want, and you may say the same. But even if I do think I have found that person, I remain willing to set aside my hopes and desires for God's best for me.

God's ways are best, and His plan for us is better than anything you or I could conjure up. He knew precisely the kind of spouse I would need before I knew I needed one. He can provide me with just the right partner for life, but I must trust Him and not lean on my limited understanding. Instead, I submit my hopes and desires before the throne of His great love and direction. "The mind of man plans his way, but the LORD directs his steps" (Proverbs 16:9, NASB). The Lord has a better way and a far better plan than I could ever hope for or presume to imagine. He knows exactly who I need, and the book of Proverbs is full of little glimpses of His wisdom and guidance. "A wife of noble character is her husband's crown, but a disgraceful wife is like decay in his bones" (Proverbs 12:4, NIV).

"Delight yourself in the LORD; And He will give you the desires of your heart" (Psalm 37:4, NASB). I submit my will and desire to the will of God so He will prepare me for what is best. I once prayed for the Lord to make me the spiritual leader for Jenna, my sidekick at the time. Little did I know the spiritual growing up I would be committing myself to over the next few years because of that request. And little did I expect that she would become the one who inspired this book. But if I leave it up to the Lord, He can deliver someone better than what I want. I don't know the future. I may have fallen in love with someone who could end up being a nightmare. I am not naive to this fact. Only God knows what is best. So I let go and let God do the picking and choosing. I not only think I have met the person that God has for me, but I've thanked God for all the ones who broke my heart by walking away. They did not leave my life—God moved them in favor of the right one. I know exactly what I want, but if God does not deliver her into my hands, He will give me someone much better.

I think of this concept as the double reward for following the Lord's direction in finding the one. Instead of dishonor and reproach, I will get twice as much in reward: "Instead of your shame, you will receive a double portion, and instead of disgrace, you will rejoice in your inheritance. And so, you will inherit a double portion in your land, and everlasting joy will be yours" (Isaiah 61:7, NIV). I know God will give me a double reward for my trouble. This promise means He will provide me with a spouse who is twice as good as I could dream up or hope to find by letting Him direct. I only have to trust in Him. God can give me far above and beyond all I could ever dare to expect, hope, or ask: "Now to him who is able to do immeasurably more than all we can ask or imagine, according to his power that is at work within us" (Ephesians 3:20, NIV).

What About Feelings?

Gary Thomas is one of my favorite authors on marriage and dating. His profound advice makes his book, *The Sacred Search,* one of my most treasured. Gary taught me that part of finding the right person to marry is becoming the right person to marry. But sad as it is, most of the women I have met are not seeking men of character as their top priority. They are seeking men whom they feel in love with at the time. According to Thomas, if she doesn't feel in love, she won't seriously consider him as a potential mate. But after marriage, she will find fault in him for the very things she overlooked as his girlfriend.

I wish I could say that most of the women I have met wanted to find a godly man with a rock-solid character, a good sense of humor, who's hardworking, and a good candidate for fatherhood. You married women know what I mean. The problem is that many chose a guy who made their hearts race and palms sweat. Perhaps this discrepancy is why so many now live with regret from romantic idealism. I understand, though. I try to consider character over feelings in my choice since one develops and changes slowly and steadily, while the other is fickle and subject to frequent change. On a lighter note, men and women are not all that different. One likes a romance novel more than fantasy football, but we're all ultimately looking for the same thing—to be loved and understood.

What About Appearance?

Many men, including myself, have made the gorgeous mistake, compounding the problem by chasing a girl down like a hound on a scent. I have learned all too well that a woman understands this already. The Bible warns us not to let a woman of beauty or charm lead us astray, for they both will fade in time: "Charm is deceptive, and beauty is fleeting; but a woman who fears the LORD is to be praised" (Proverbs 31:30, NIV). When choosing a wife, I now put more emphasis on things that last; a woman's body goes through more rapid changes than her character. As a man, it is easy to feel romantic love toward a physically attractive woman, but her physical appearance is the thing most likely to change. I have not let sexual attraction sweep me away to the altar. I try to use wisdom in decision-making rather than let my feelings motivate me. But for many people I have met, putting this into practice is analogous to saying you're going to start a diet after eating an entire pizza—seriously.

I also don't expect the selfish side of the woman I desire to change before marriage. Her self-centeredness is the least likely thing to change. And *The Sacred Search* has led me to conclude that if she is promiscuous or too physical in dating, I expect that to kill intimacy after marriage, so I will avoid it. When it comes to sex, virtue will be our friend. It might shock you as much as it woke me up when I read Gary's sound advice: "Your best chance at sexual satisfaction in marriage is not to focus on appearance alone, but rather to find a woman of virtue." Proverbs 31 describes this kind of righteous woman. She is a woman who will be a kind, compassionate, and forgiving person. She will be a wife who is giving and a satisfying sexual partner. I am sure the same is true for men as well.

I have often asked myself if I am ready, internalizing the nuances of it all. When I answer yes, the next question is: *Am I sure?* Once I marry, I know I need to be prepared to see the same face every night before I go to sleep, and it will be the first one I will see every morning. Her body will please or bore me. Her words will encourage or discourage me. Will we build a life and career together, will we work separately, or will she depend on me? Will we make a life together with a purpose and mission or, at some point, get bored with each other? "The consequences of making a foolish choice can be painful and lasting," says Gary Thomas in *The Sacred Search*. "I cannot overstate how crucial it is to be cautious and discerning in making such an important decision," he adds. I want a future that holds tears of joy, not regret.

I don't want to get married only for the sake of not being single. I have enjoyed being single for the most part. Not experiencing divorce, like so many I know, has been an incredible blessing. But I have grown up. I now welcome the thought of marriage because God considers it a good thing. He also compares a good wife's value to that of precious jewels. I want that treasure. I embrace it for the companionship, the partnership, the love, the devotion, and all the favor God is referring to that I am missing out on in Proverbs 18:22 as a single man. The last thing I want to experience is divorce, but I don't want to miss out on God's best. And I do not want to base my decision on appearance. Nonetheless, many I know have done just that.

What's God's Ideal?

It took me a while, but I needed to submit my ideal spouse to God's best for me. In return, He informed me what she should look like as a potential spouse. The first half of Proverbs 31:10 (NIV) asks, "A wife of noble character who can find?" This question was tough to answer when most men like me are initially drawn to a woman by her outward appearance. "…For the LORD does not see as man sees; for a man looks at the outward appearance, but the LORD looks at the heart" (1 Samuel 16:7, NKJV). Coming from a career based primarily on outward looks only intensified my misplaced mindset with physical influence over inner beauty.

Jenna's outward exterior is what got my initial attention years earlier, but it was her inner beauty that altered my immature mindset, allowing God to change my way of thinking over time and extol her virtues. From day one, she was someone who would not model anything sheer or too revealing, liberating women from being seen only as sex objects. Jenna religiously slept with a pocket Bible tucked in her bra over her heart at night. She considered herself a Christian and attended the same Catholic church for many years, from which her parents even had the priest over for dinner. Most important to me was a childlike innocence about her that I respected, thinking back on my fourth-grade self. She did not sleep around and frowned upon the thought of women who did so. And she did not take any gobbledygook from Silicon Valley men who hit on her while working for Makara. Politically and morally savvy, she was clever enough to smoke out trickery. She was all about family loyalty, honoring her parents, and loving children. She was intelligent, well-educated, ambitious, and always wanting to learn new things to better herself and others. These were just some of the many godly qualities that attracted her to me, making up for our occasional differences in music genre preferences.

It takes a man of God-given wisdom to see beyond the superficial and seek a capable and virtuous woman. He looks for intelligence and integrity over bosom and fading beauty. I finally desired to be that kind of man. The rest of Proverbs 31:10, along with verses 11–12, says, "An excellent wife is more precious than jewels." And it is comforting to read, "The heart of her husband trusts her." It also states, "She will do him good and not harm all the days of his life." What a perfect picture of marriage and an excellent example for those like me seeking to be an ideal spouse.

What About Experience?

I've had some concerns about my potential mate's sexual experience. I want to avoid regretful comparisons. Unfortunately, I know from experience. I gained this knowledge before I got more serious about relinquishing my wants for God's best. It was as if I had taken a bite of the forbidden fruit from the tree of "it's best you not know." Although I remained a virgin longer than most, I experienced good and bad sex after that and now know the difference. Knowing what I know could have set me up for surefire failure in marriage if my future wife or I weren't spot-on perfect. Since that is impossible, it took a lot of character development with God's intervention to realize the error of my ways. Since then, I have relinquished my expectations in favor of a godly mate.

1 Peter 3:7 instructs me as a husband to love and honor my future wife in an understanding way. God has been preparing me to be that for my future spouse so that I won't compare anyone to her. With a little wisdom and brokenhearted experience under my belt, I now have a new view of men. If he isn't going to marry her, he should take his hands off another man's future! No one has given him jurisdiction to interfere or play with another man's destiny. He is waging war against his soul by his own doings (see 1 Peter 2:11). As for me, I finally submitted to the answer to how a man can keep his way pure. The answer is clear: "…By keeping it according to Thy word. Thy word I have treasured in my heart, That I may not sin against Thee" (Psalm 119:9, 11, NASB 1977).

I prefer to buy something new rather than used and broken. I could say similar about me not wanting someone else sleeping with my future spouse. This kind of past is not an area of life in which I ideally prefer my future spouse to have had a lot of experience, though nowadays, that is rare and expecting a lot. It hurts loving someone who has, especially when she has chosen someone over me. *The Bachelor's* fantasy suite may make intriguing television drama, but in the real world, its honest end is regret. I do not fool myself into thinking otherwise. Sex is a gift from God, not a present for a boyfriend. While this may too be hard for others to endeavor, I plan to be pure in this area for myself in loving obedience to God and pray she will as well.

What About Fidelity?

I have learned a lot about fidelity in marriage from listening to more married women than I can count in over thirty years of business and two years working for Makara. Make no mistake about it—a bad marriage is like a nightmare with no morning to come, which I heard loud and clear from these women. Their words inspired me to plaster an Old Testament passage in my mind, if not its own fidelity plaque on my wall, to stay true and faithful when I get married one day. Directed at men like me, the last verse of the passage confirms who is always watching even when my wife is not. If I don't fear the Lord more than my future wife after reading it, I won't fear cheating on her.

> Drink water from your own cistern, running water from your own well. Should your springs overflow in the streets, your streams of water in the public squares? Let them be yours alone, never to be shared with strangers. May your fountain be blessed, and may you rejoice in the wife of your youth. A loving doe, a graceful deer—may her breasts satisfy you always, may you ever be intoxicated with her love. Why, my son, be intoxicated with another man's wife? Why embrace the bosom of a wayward

woman? For your ways are in full view of the Lord, and he examines all your paths.

Proverbs 5:15–21 (NIV)

If I could add any words to this in today's language, I would ask all men to join me and inscribe the following into our skulls. Please don't take her for granted or disrespect her in word, deed, or thought. She was once worth more than fine gold in our eyes.

"If a man wants a woman to behave like an angel, he must first create heaven on earth for her" is not a Bible verse. It is a self-centered, selfish statement made by someone lacking noble character. But as a godly man, I will need to use all my power to cherish my wife as a tender doe, treating her like a princess. For a wife of noble character is worth far more than rubies (see Proverbs 31:10). As a gentleman, if I am fortunate enough to land Mrs. Right, I will treat her appropriately, remembering who blessed me with her in the first place: "Houses and wealth are inherited from parents, but a prudent wife is from the Lord" (Proverbs 19:14, NIV). It turns out she is God's gift to me, after all! (See Genesis 2:22.) And if I ever have children, the best thing I can do for them is to love their mother.

There is one thing Jenna will never do if she is honest with herself—she will never complain about how I treated her. The ring story was only one little example of that kind of treatment. I am not perfect, that is for sure, but I am faithful in deed and thought. I do not take her for granted or disrespect her when she is with me or out of sight. I know how to practice respect and faithfulness even before there is a commitment. I also enjoy the peace of mind that comes from doing so when she is not around or not doing likewise. Because of all these things, I know she will always compare other men to me and the standards I set by the way I treated her. With fond memories of my treatment for her, others will never measure up, and Jenna will always return to me.

Am I Learning?

I experienced a day of destiny in my youth. Someone accused my best Christian friend in high school of sleeping with a girl who had an interest in both of us. She pursued us both with relentless abandon for years. I did not believe her when she informed me of his transgression. There was no way. I was adamant in defense of my friend in the face of her repeated, sincere, consistent story. My friend and I were members of the school's Christian club, and he dropped out of sports his senior year to devote more of his time and life to the Lord and study of the Bible. I imagined him becoming a pastor one day and looked up to him as a Christian and a leader. We went to the youth group together on weekends, where we prayed and worshiped. We attended Bible studies together during the week. This girl's story was no doubt false. I even told him so. One day, my friend came over to my parents' house while they were at work. I'll never forget his humble posture as I sat in the living room listening to him tell me her story was true. I don't remember anything after that. It was such an unexpected and devastating revelation. All I know is that he looked broken, and I was shell-shocked.

That incident left an impression on me for the next ten years. It was a day of destiny that left me determined never to have that conversation with my future wife. And I was ever so grateful to God for His mercy. He loved me enough to spare my heart from the early emotional and spiritual agony I saw in my friend that day. I thanked the Lord for the good fortune of allowing me to learn from another's mistake.

What's My Record?

I remained a virgin until twenty-six and said no a thousand times in my secular career. But I was far from perfect, for the modeling business provided many opportunities for wrongdoing. I received many offers and experienced so much temptation that there was a running joke between my best friend and me at the time. Of course I would dress up as Hugh Hefner at Halloween—who else would I be? Not that I admired the man for all the women he bedded or the life he led—I didn't. I wish I could say I've been a model of faith and moral prudence for the Lord since then and offered that as a gift to my future spouse, but who am I fooling? I've had some epic fails along the way. But as a more earnest Christian now, I can at least say that I have been saving myself for only my future wife the past several years.

Even working for Makara brought on solicitations from some of her female customers. One flat-out told me, "I could set you up with Heather (not her real name) if you like." Heather and I had already hit it off as good friends, and she was quite the catch. If it were not for Jenna, I might have conceded; instead, I turned down her offer. More than once, another customer threw her arms around me and attempted to kiss me with the thrust of a Mentos candy in a Diet Coke. She also told me she could not stop thinking about me. Another customer passed me a note communicating her sister wanted me to ask her out. Still another woman came into the business and would not leave my side until someone with her said to me, "She has the hots for you." My admirer then retreated in embarrassment. Even a mother mentioned that her attractive daughter was recently single when she noticed our amiable conversation about things other than Makara's business.

Makara was aware of all the attention I was getting and how I remained loyal to the one I held onto in my heart and for our future. Not accepting even a kiss from anyone other than the girl I had in mind was one of many things that kept me true to Jenna years before she ever knew. Why put off until tomorrow what I can do today? I don't need more sexual experience, nor does my future wife. She may not please her current boyfriend, but she will please God. Her boyfriend isn't the one she will answer to when this life is over.

There is only one kind of safe sex for me, in my opinion. If I am going to make love to the person I am in love with, I can do so wearing the most reliable thing—a wedding ring. I don't want to compare my spouse to others with whom I have been intimate. I know I'll regret it! So I do the right thing for myself in this area. When my sin is in the field of sex, I not only sin against God and my future spouse, but I also sin against myself: "Flee from sexual immorality. All other sins a person commits are outside the body, but whoever sins sexually, sins against their own body" (1 Corinthians 6:18, NIV).

What About Jenna?

Although I have sounded as if my mind were made up in my writing, as if Jenna was Amanda Jordan singing "I Choose You," I am trusting God for the right one. I know that God has a perfect plan for me and the ideal person to walk together with through this life. When it happens, I will be ready, having learned from Jenna that a successful relationship with any woman will ground itself in her knowing that she shines brighter than him. So I wait on God to bring a mate of His choosing rather than wrestle with the reality that He knows better than me, and I needed His help. God's ways are so much higher, and His standards are far superior to my criteria for a spouse anyway.

Trusting God's plan and His timing frees me from many emotional cares and worries that prevent me from enjoying life. So I lay my hopes on the altar of God's selection. A life and spouse worth having are a life and spouse worth the wait. I know that one day, someone of God's choosing is going to come along and appreciate everything about me. That someone else will treasure what Jenna took for granted. "Some of the best things in life are lost when they are standing right in front of you," as my mom would say.

Letting God Lead

My future spouse is in God's hands, so I trust God for big dreams. I leave it in God's hands when it comes to finding the one. A woman of God is someone worth waiting for, so I am patient. God knows what is best for me, so I let go and let God do the choosing and expect a double reward. He knows the kind of spouse I need, so I trust Him. One day, I will thank God for all the ones who broke my heart before her. It will be my double reward for following the Lord's direction in finding the one.

While waiting, I will become the right person to marry as well. I will walk in God's ways before the wedding as a preparation for marriage and continue to learn from the mistakes of others. I will become the person that God designed me to be even if I must give up some things. I will wait for a Proverbs 31 woman while being an Ephesians 5 man, so that we can have a 1 Corinthians 13 kind of love. I do this before marriage in preparation to pray with my spouse, kneeling at the foot of our bed.

"Houses and wealth are inherited from parents, but a prudent wife is from the Lord" (Proverbs 19:14, NIV).

CHAPTER 12: SOULMATE

"A wife of noble character who can find? She is worth far more than rubies" (Proverbs 31:10, NIV).

While at the gym one day, I revealed to Jenna my realization that I knew I liked her as more than a friend when I saw her dancing there that first day of June. Even though I thought I was being honest, the truth is that it started to develop much sooner—I just hadn't realized it. I was smitten way back when we first danced together at my sister's wedding. Jenna's adorable little step, rhythm, coordination, agility, and dance moves to the music's beat left me in adoration. Perhaps her previous elite cheerleading experience from when she was in school bolstered her eloquent moves and inimitable style. My mind was spellbound, mesmerized, and lost in the translation of interpreting the language through myriad nuances of attraction. That smile all the way through had won me over before I knew what hit me. To me, she was the human equivalent of Classic Coke—great with vanilla or cherry and perfect with my favorite food.

Jenna unwittingly either discovered or unmasked her physical attraction to me as well at the gym. After finishing her cardio and weight workout, she found me in the pool area only to catch me finishing up the last lap of my swim. As I pushed off the pool floor and exited my lap lane vertically, Jenna froze in her tracks several feet from me, gazed at my upper body while standing still and caught off guard.

"Whoa," was her exact and only verbal outburst, as if pleasantly surprised.

Her unexpected reaction reassured me with confidence that everything she saw within my spirit as a potential soulmate was now bolstered by her realization of physical attraction toward me as well. If our story had started or ended at that moment, we would only be recollecting amorous lust or admiration at best, but we already had fifteen months of close friendship under our belt. As our friendship bond grew over the years, it became clear that we were becoming something akin to soulmates. The keyword is "becoming," for it was not "destined" from the beginning of time but instead developed over time. Given the right conditions, it could have progressed with someone else, but it didn't. Jenna appeared to be my soulmate.

"Happily ever after" fairy tales like "Sleeping Beauty" and "Snow White" are romantic notions that are not in the Bible. The Bible never mentions the word "soulmate," but from the text, it's clear that my biblical soulmate is simply the person I choose to marry. So, the idea that God designed one specific person for me as a soulmate, whom I can never be happy apart from, is not biblical. This line of thinking can make one think that we are incomplete until we find our soulmate, a trap I sometimes fell victim to with Jenna. It led to feelings of loneliness, as I described in the "Holiday" chapter. God has not saved one perfect person for us since the beginning to make imperfect us complete. It's a romantic notion to think of Jenna as predestined for me when Jesus is the only one who makes me whole and complete.

Now, this is not to say that God is not concerned about whom I marry. If God cares enough to know the number of hairs on my head and values me more than many sparrows (see Luke 12:7), it is a safe bet that God profoundly cares about whom I marry. I have found the one my soul loves, so when I refer to a soulmate, I am referring to "the one" I want to marry. The idea of a soulmate puts me in danger of mistaking passion and feelings for the commitment to come. I know the basis of a lasting godly marriage choice starts with a promise maintained through dedication, not attraction or feelings. So if I truly think I may have found the one, there are a few things I need to share before I take the plunge.

Ten Premarital Preparations

Long ago I may have been the naïve guy at a strip club who thought the dancers really fancied him. My business made me wise up. My relationship with Jenna made me grow up and the Lord led me to look up. As a godly man now, I will court a woman after serious contemplation and spiritual consideration and will approach God before I ever pursue her. I fell for someone different than me. I'm drawn toward people unlike me because I need them to balance me. But there are certain things we should not differ in and should agree on before marriage. Ten hold value to me before I tie the knot. I know some may seem extreme and challenging, but I only share what I already did myself once I decided to get serious about my walk with the Lord. These ten listed are in order of least to most important for me. They are things that I value to be good practice before marriage.

- 10. I will love my potential spouse's family as my own. As a typical single person, I spent holidays with my family. My wife will spend them with my family as well as I with her relatives. After all, I will be the one asking her to marry me and not vice versa.

- 9. I won't drink since she doesn't. Unless she encourages it for a special occasion, I will do as she does. It would be disrespectful and reveal that a singleness mentality remains in me to do otherwise.

- 8. I will put the interests of my future spouse before my own (see Philippians 2:3–4). I once thought marriage was 50/50. It's not. I will enter this union ready to put my spouse first (after the Lord), especially being the man. I hope to achieve this by learning, then practicing, her love languages, as Gary Chapman teaches about in his book, *The 5 Love Languages*.

- 7. I will stay out of debt prior to marriage, encouraging her to do similarly. After marriage, we will continue doing so as a team. As a man, God not only expects me to be the spiritual leader in moral issues but also in financial matters. Staying out of debt is one way I can set an example for my future spouse.

- 6. I will marry someone who fears God as I do. Choosing a spouse is also choosing and accepting my future. If she doesn't fall on her knees in prayer, she doesn't deserve for me to fall on one knee with a ring for her. God will not bless our relationship unless we involve Him in it.

- 5. I will be honest and encouraging in our communication: "Truthful lips endure forever, but a lying tongue lasts only a moment" (Proverbs 12:19, NIV). Eight little interwoven muscles make up the tongue, but it can break hearts big time. I must be careful, truthful, and uplifting with my words.

- 4. I want to marry my best friend, the one who makes me fall in love with God every day. If she doesn't love Jesus, I won't date her. It will only be harder ending the relationship later. If she isn't a follower of Jesus, she should not have been my closest friend in the first place.

- 3. We will study the Bible together, finding verses of mutual interest to memorize together so that we may be careful to do according to all that is written in it, for then we will be prosperous and successful according to Joshua 1:8. "Seek first the kingdom of God and His righteousness, and all these things will be added to you" (Matthew 6:33, ESV). We will build our relationship around Christ being in the center.

- 2. We will be abstinent together before marriage and then physically and mentally faithful after (see Exodus 20:14). As a man, this next verse is tailor-made for me: "I say, anyone who even looks at a woman with lust has already committed adultery with her in his heart" (Matthew 5:28, NLT).

- 1. We will pray and worship on our knees together whenever possible. We will pray before each meal together, holding hands, which I learned from Jenna. We'll pray together so we remain together, and if she leaves, it will give her one more reason to return. (Did you know that sea otters hold hands when they sleep so they don't drift apart?)

The Best Part

Do you pray with your spouse, significant other, or close friends? Do you get down on your knees together and pray? Let me testify to its value by recounting an endearing moment I shared with Jenna. We knelt in prayer at the end of her bed in my guestroom during the Christmas season. There was a moment when she leaned her head against my shoulder as I prayed in earnest concerning her family. It was not a special prayer for me. I've prayed similarly for her and her family many times in private, unbeknownst to her. It is quite fantastic and beautiful when someone prays for you without you knowing.

There are fewer forms of more profound and purer love. But this time, we shared it as of one accord together. It bonded us and revealed what she could expect with me as her spiritual leader one day. It was one of the best moments of our relationship, and I treasure the thought of it. It was a bonding experience that made me want to make this a regular part of our routine. If the man in your life isn't the wise, godly example you'd want to lead you, how much of an asset would he be as a father to your precious children? Finding a man you can lean on as your spiritual rock is better than being a babysitter to the guy who comes home from work after stopping off at the bar, strip club, fantasy football team meeting, or coed gym of younger, primped women, more fit than you. Let's be real: going on websites you don't know about is more likely to be on this guy's mind than prayer.

You may have heard the saying, "Those who pray together stay together." I don't know if you want that, but I sure do! I will marry someone who prays for me and is willing to pray with me for the rest of her life. God's ways and plans are much better than mine. He loved me enough to send His only son to die for me, so it only makes sense that He would have the best intentions for me. That includes me and my significant other coming to Him together this way.

The Outward Beauty

To my female readers, please be patient and bear with me as I share some stereotypical views. These words on outward beauty were something I spoke in a conversation with Makara. She suggested that I share them with others. I hope you will take them with a grain of salt and chuckle for a moment. It may give you some perspective amid a heavy subject. It will be brief. I promise. As a male, I wish someone wiser would have shared this with me long ago.

I was like a broken toy after getting discarded after landing a beautiful woman. Whether I realized it or not, one way or another, a beautiful woman always seems to get her way. When I got involved with a beautiful woman, I had no idea what I was up against. I never imagined everyone telling her how adorable she was as a child. I never imagined boys always telling her how pretty she was and competing for her attention. I never imagined every guy telling her how beautiful she was after high school. I never imagined men continually hitting on her or wealthy men always trying to buy her. These are some of the problems of a beautiful woman, including Jenna. For some fortunate or inauspicious reason, I have worked with many beautiful women. For thirty-plus years, they have come from all over the U.S. and Canada, sharing their hopes and dreams with me.

CHAPTER 12: SOULMATE

The reason thousands of women have come to me over the years is not because of any particular words of advice I could give them on dating or men. Quite the opposite; I received a great deal of knowledge from their heartbreaks. The reason was to help them fulfill their dreams of modeling. But unbeknownst to them, the wisdom they gave me far outweighed what I gave them. Most of these women, but not all, were pretty, and many were quite beautiful. Their words of experience on this matter were better than mine. I learned that the typical beautiful woman is not going to care about my comfort level. She is the kind of woman who has never or rarely heard the word "no." Much of what she has came on the heels of a silver platter. So I shouldn't expect her to care about my feelings, much less my broken heart. This problem is something we men have created.

Yes, this is a case where women must receive credit for being so much brighter than us men. One bit of advice I got about beautiful women is, "Love them, but be careful if you want to marry one of them." It's not her fault, but a beautiful woman will always have something over a nice guy. Unlike me, she has hardly ever, or never, faced rejection. If broken over beauty is a familiar feeling in that male heart of yours, think more like a woman. A woman is more likely to look at the inside of a person when it comes to relationships. We men are often too visual, and women know this. They are more mature than most of us for a reason.

I have heard so much from beautiful women: they are often the most lonely and insecure because men are afraid to approach them, not willing to risk rejection. Thank you, women, for your patience through that little rant.

I Got Educated

By choice I went unloved rather than disrespected for years. Most of the women I have met, given an option, would go disrespected rather than unloved. So the next time I am feeling disrespected, I will consider if I am making my woman feel unloved or not adored. As for respect, I got educated on what women want from men. A woman wants a man she can respect. As a man of God who is a leader, I could be that kind of guy. And if I wanted to be a quality catch, I needed to know a woman's emotional and psychological needs.

My business familiarized me with things like depression and self-esteem issues women face. Feelings of inadequacy and lack of confidence were common among many of these women. Financial issues were a top concern for most women I have met in my career. Menstrual and physiological problems women face were a mystery to me as a single man starting a company. Insecurities about aging and losing outward beauty were a common source of concern for so many female models I have met over the years. Problems that arose from bearing and raising children were unfamiliar to me early on, so I needed to learn some basics to navigate the emotional road of understanding a woman.

I've learned that I need to assure my soulmate of her beauty by telling her how attractive she is with or without makeup. Her countenance and eyes will reflect that of a cherished prize. I will remind her how adorable she looks in sweats or beautiful in that evening dress. I will open her car door and seat her first in the restaurant every time. I will show love with consistency. I will hold my tongue rather than raising my voice at her and consider my failings before criticizing her character. I will value her opinions, her preferences, and what makes her happy. If she loves shopping like Jenna, I will take her to get what she wants. It does not have to be expensive to show her that I care and trust her judgment. It beats a broken heart any day. And the last thing I will ever do is disrespect her with my eyes on that device or other woman when talking to her.

Awaiting Women's Approval

Having seen the worst side of men in my career has left me with many concerns. If I am blessed enough to have a daughter one day, I will have ten suggestions on men, dating, and marriage for her:

- 10. Wait for God's Mr. Right, and let God choose your mate. From this one decision will come 90 percent of all your happiness or misery. Never confuse a lesson for a soulmate. And remember something, sweetheart: There is a big difference between a godly man and a religious man. Don't wait on the Lord for the only one that pays attention to you. Wait for the one paying attention to what God is telling Him when it comes to you. And don't only wait for the right one; pray for the right one. "Women, you are not rehabilitation centers for badly raised men. It's not your job to fix him, change him, parent, or raise him. You want a partner, not a project," says Julia Roberts.

- 9. God loves you, so trust Him in your waiting. God is love, so it only makes sense that you should go through Him to find the one that you should marry. The one God is sending your way will be so amazing that he will make you forget you ever had a broken heart. He will hug you so tight that all your broken pieces will fit back together.

- 8. Your suitor's effort will prove his interest in you. Always remember, someone's effort is a surefire reflection of their interest in you. Any man can treat you right when he's with you, but the revealing of his real character often happens when you are not with him.

- 7. Faith and faithfulness are fundamental. "Rich or handsome?" a girl asked. "Loyal," a woman replied. Women can't make a man faithful. When a man's devotion is to God, his commitment will be to her as well. If a man loves a woman's soul, he will end up loving one woman. But if he only loves a woman's body or face, all the women in the world won't be satisfying enough for him. If you doubt that, study the writings of Solomon and the life of Hugh Hefner.

- 6. Learn the word no. Your decision to abstain from sex until marriage is between you and God. He will not send any person who is out to change your mind about that, period. A woman's purity is a sacred thing. If a man does not value or desire to protect it until marriage, he's not the one. True love honors and protects.

- 5. Pay attention to what matters in the long run. Those things include humility, gentleness, patience, kindness, and truthfulness. You should want someone who is attentive, generous, responsible, dependable, and who uses discretion. These are the character qualities found in a man of God. You are an emotional being. Will your Prince Charming be sensitive to that? Expect to land a man with wandering eyes and a wayward mind if all you seek is tall, dark, and handsome.

- 4. Take a good look at yourself. Sure, men are visual creatures with different opinions on beauty and physical attraction, but you are not auditioning for a Victoria's Secret photoshoot. Wise men know that beauty is fleeting and notice how much you rely on your exterior. It's not all about looks. Deep down, they also want someone with a big heart, some ambition, and who is fun and playful. They also observe the way you treat people you don't know. If all you like doing is looking in the mirror, staring at your phone, and going shopping, what do you have to offer a quality man?

- 3. Marry a man after God's own heart. I agree with a saying I once read: "A woman's heart should be so lost in God that a man must seek God to find her." This kind of noble spouse is what you should want because a man after God's heart will know how to lead your heart. But sometimes the person you want doesn't deserve you. So marry someone who helps you fall in love with God every day (see 2 Corinthians 6:14). Imagine a relationship where you both love and worship God together. You should want a unified relationship where people look at the two of you and say, "God put them together."

- 2. Little things do matter. Does your prospect dislike animals, break promises, or give you secondary treatment? Does he use excuses, smoke, or lie? Is he lazy and always broke? Does he spend all his free time in the gym or clubs? A good man supports you in your endeavors. He adds a sense of calm to your life. He listens to you and makes sacrifices for your happiness. He's always available to make time for the two of you and has no problem making spontaneous plans for you. He treats his mother well and makes you feel beautiful even on your worst days. He holds you in high esteem and shows you he loves you with or without words. He opens your door, and you feel you're his priority. He wants to spend holidays with you and talks about your future. Yes, these little things matter. Don't blame a clown for acting like a clown. Blame yourself for going to the circus.

- 1. Last, here are a few things your suitor may say to you if he is a keeper:
    - o 1. You are beautiful inside and out.
    - o 2. I love your smile.
    - o 3. What do you think?
    - o 4. I support you, or I've got your back.
    - o 5. I'll take care of this for you.
    - o 6. I'm sorry.
    - o 7. I understand.
    - o 8. You're so funny.
    - o 9. I trust you.
    - o 10. I miss you.

At this point, you might think number 1 should be "I love you." I suppose it could be, but it's not. That's because it is much better if he shows you he loves you rather than tells you. You may want to hear it, but actions speak louder than words in love and romance. Most women know this to be true, but they crave the words. Actions matter most.

All these points assume her potential suitor is spiritually mature enough (which includes being able to handle conflict, doesn't lie, and isn't selfish), all things I learned while attending a service on dating at Cornerstone Church in Chandler, Arizona. It also assumes the possible mate is emotionally healthy (which includes being able to control anger, having a healthy self-esteem, and understanding authority), which were additional important considerations preached at that session.

Since my daughter is likely to have high aspirations, allow me to add this final tidbit. It is from none other than Marilyn Monroe: "Women who seek to be equal with men lack ambition." Take it from someone who has heard the saying "All men are dogs" a thousand times and knows it is not valid. But such generalizations as this have some basis in truth. I have owned popular websites that cater to men and have listened to thousands of women, so I have seen and heard it all. I understand men, but I respect women and empathize with them.

I draw near the end of this subject from underneath the covers of my cozy bed on a crisp winter's morning. My cat, snuggling with me, lies curled up, sleeping between my feet. Having already prayed on my knees at my bedside earlier this morning, I will share an intimate part of it with you. It is something I have spoken to the Lord a thousand times if I have uttered these words once.

Single Soul's Prayer

Thank You, Lord, that he who finds a wife finds a good thing and obtains favor from You (Proverbs 18:22). I want that kind of favor. Thank You, Lord, for Your undeserving, divine favor that is upon me. I call upon those things that are not as though they were and claim them over my future wife (Romans 4:17). For all things are possible with God. What is impossible with man is possible with God (Luke 18:27). Thank You, Lord, that You are binding Satan in my future wife's life and building a hedge of thorns around her (Hosea 2:6). Thank You for protecting her from the evil one. Thank You, Lord, that You are drawing her to You and then to me in Your perfect timing. Thank You, Lord, that You are making a way when there seems to be no way (Isaiah 43:16). Thank You, Lord, for the plans You have for me and her—plans to prosper me and not harm me, plans to give me hope and a future (Jeremiah 29:11). Thank You, Lord, that my wife will experience that even more with me than on her own. Thank You, Lord, that You have a good plan for me. Thank You, Lord, that You are healing my heart, restoring my soul, and making me whole. Thank You, Lord, that You are working behind the scenes in ways I do not know, see, or understand, but You are working. Thank You, Lord, that whatever I ask for in prayer and believe, trust, and am confident in that You will grant it (Mark 11:24). Thank You, Lord, that even though my mind plans its way, You direct my steps (Proverbs 16:9). Thank You, Lord, that You will instruct me and teach me which way I should go and counsel me with Your loving eye upon me (Psalm 32:8). Thank You, Lord, that You are leading and guiding me in the direction You want me to go.

Thank You, Lord, for Your goodness, kindness, and faithfulness, in Jesus' name, Amen.

"An excellent wife is the crown of her husband..." (Proverbs 12:4, NASB).

CHAPTER 13: EXCELLENCE

"Then this Daniel became distinguished above all the other high officials and satraps, because an excellent spirit was in him. And the king planned to set him over the whole kingdom" (Daniel 6:3, ESV).

It was a typical weekend night working for Makara's business, not knowing but wondering when I would see or work with Jenna next. I recall going to the men's restroom and getting distracted by seeing a quarter on the floor by the toilet. Someone must have dropped it when using the facilities. Being scrupulous when it comes to detail, I stared at it for a moment. I imagined it was full of germs in this unsanitary environment. I worked here for free. I didn't even keep the tips; I gave them to Makara, who owned the business, or Jenna if she showed up. Why was this meaningless coin drawing my attention? I've always been a staunch saver and someone who doesn't like to waste anything, but God had another plan in this instance that would lead to a story and lesson. It would make me a more quality person and a better leader for Jenna.

CHAPTER 13: EXCELLENCE

I left the bathroom but later returned to use it again and saw the coin still there—albeit I feigned to ignore it. This time I picked up it with a paper towel then washed it even though it was shiny and new to the eye. After placing it in my pocket, I soon forgot about it. When I got home that night, a sense of guilt gripped me. I'd never taken a penny from this place even though I had earned thousands for others. So why did I leave with a quarter that was not mine? Unbeknownst to anyone, I returned to work the next day with the quarter and slipped it into the register without Jenna or Makara noticing. What a peaceful feeling! I have failed the excellence test many times, but this was not one of them. I was aware that Luke 16:10 (NIV) says, "Whoever can be trusted with very little can also be trusted with much, and whoever is dishonest with very little will also be dishonest with much." So, I had to do my best to "maintain always a blameless conscience both before God and before men," as Acts 24:16 (NASB1995) says.

When broken, you want a clear and blameless conscience so you can live in peace with God. Learning how to live a life of excellence over time was one more sanding off of the rough edges in my heart. So let my shared, unmasked mistakes and triumphs save you heartache as you travel with me down the road of untangled lessons I learned about excellence.

Little Things Matter

I recall another day having lunch at a grocery store with a friend and the store's manager after church. Sitting face to face as we ate, my friend told me that the manager had mentioned something to her in jest that opened my eyes to excellence. He told her how he observed that I would sometimes snack on a few goji berries while shopping. That didn't sit well with me—sensing an unusual truculent mindset overtaking me. I spent thousands of dollars a year at that overpriced store, and yet I was immediately convicted. Even though it would seem like such a minor offense to most people, my wrongdoing was revealing to me. Snacking and making free samples out of a few nuts and dried fruit was something many people did. I asked myself, *What is the big deal?* That question seemed to forebode a critical moment on the horizon.

The answer came immediately. God reminded me again of something I had learned from Terri Savelle Foy and Joyce Meyer. I had asked God for much, especially when it came to my hopes and dreams of a future with Jenna. Did I want it or not? I was never going to be able to write about excellence with integrity and how it better prepared me to be a godly leader or potential spouse for Jenna or someone else if I had none in the hidden areas of my own life. Then I realized that God rewards us in public for what we do in private (see Matthew 6:6). And how we act and what we do in private are much more important than how we behave and what we do in public.

God sees everything and is watching and observing the little things in our lives. That is because our future always has a connection to what is happening now. Most people would not even give a second thought to this way of thinking. But I can assure you that God has me up at 2 a.m. writing about this unseen and overlooked topic for a reason. The reason is that excellence in little things matters to God if I wish to be free from my brokenness. Excellence plays a crucial role in healing, and it was a prerequisite for where God wanted to take me, with or without Jenna. So I ended this sampling habit I once thought of as no big deal.

CHAPTER 13: EXCELLENCE

Distinction Is Excellent

I want to be a person of excellence, which means I should be someone who practices integrity and God-fearing moral distinction. Excellence is not something I think about every day. It shouldn't be. It should come as natural as giving or doing good, even though living with excellence can be a struggle for some because it doesn't take much to veer off track. Keeping your head and heart in the right place can be a constant battle. If I ever had hoped to be an irreplaceable spouse rather than a statistic, I need to be a person of excellence. If I aspire to be a friend whom others trust and respect more than their other friends, I need to be a person of distinction. If I desire to be someone who loves their neighbor as themselves, as it says in Matthew 22:39, I need to be a person of excellence. If I ever want to have a profession that people respect, I better be a person of distinction.

When I wasn't running my own business, being a person of distinction meant I never displayed a lackadaisical attitude when covering for Jenna at Makara's company, regardless of my *gratis* status. I served her customers rapidly and set them up for an experience that was never dull or commonplace but distinctive. It meant I was always kind, considerate, and mindful that I was there to help Makara and make Jenna's load lighter. Being distinctive made me want to assist Jenna to the best of my ability by making her skills stand out among the other employees and look top-notch for the customers.

"You take their orders, and I'll help make your drinks," I told Jenna.

"Good idea, Michael."

"And I'll take the orders from the new tables in the back for you so you can have both the back and front tables," I said.

"Thank you, Michael."

I remember the excitement we shared over $50 and $80 tips I got for her from one customer, then another. It was a sheer joy helping her succeed and look good doing it, while helping pay for medical expenses and basic bills to survive independently. It was something I needed to carry on in all aspects of my life.

No one remembers the ex-husband or ex-wife with fondness. No one misses the selfish, self-centered friend who only thought of themselves. And no one wants to help care for the yard or bring in the groceries for the neighbor who could care less about them. But a person of excellence does. A person of distinction keeps their word even at a cost. A person of excellence is upright and loyal in secret when no one is looking at or praising them and doesn't cut in line or cut people off on the road. And this individual doesn't roll the car window down to throw out a piece of trash or spit out their gum. A person of excellence is conscientious, especially when it comes to working. This person completes the task or job at hand and does not leave the work for someone else to finish.

This person goes beyond the requirements, leaving the next one in line or who takes over better off and does not claim or seek unemployment benefits while working. A person of distinction is aware that God hears every word that comes out of their mouth, including, "I don't know—and I don't care." Their speech reflects their knowledge of this. (See Ephesians 4:29, 5:4 and Colossians 3:18.) Not that I did, but I could swear and cuss all I wanted, unless I desired for others to think of me as a person of excellence or to hold me in high esteem. It is also one reason no one ever heard a negative word come out of my mouth about Jenna, regardless of how much her words or actions may have hurt me. These are only some of the things I need to be if I want to be a person of distinction.

CHAPTER 13: EXCELLENCE

Striving to be a person of distinction motivated me to show up early to work for Makara whenever possible. Sure, I was there to cover for Jenna if she did not show up, was unable to come to work, or unabashedly strolled in late with a smile. Still, the desire for excellence sparked the discipline for me to arrive early or be available unexpectedly so Jenna would never look bad. I wanted her to look like a princess and, to be more exact, my perfect princess.

It reminded me of an incident that happened when at the airport, traveling with Jenna. A woman before us got in the way of Jenna or her space, almost bumping Jenna apparently without realizing it. Jenna's sigh of annoyance and fidgeting through noticeable anger caught me off guard. I wanted to remove the observation from memory but often struggled with how her reaction left a festering blemish of disappointment in my mind. I so wanted others to see her as a woman of distinction, humility, and grace with the elegance of a queen waving her white-gloved palm to the crowd. Instead, that day, she demonstrated the self-centered pride and apathy of a monarch who thinks everyone is below her. The realization was a bitter pill to swallow, concealed in the protective dungeon of rose-colored memories locked up with my dirty little secret flaws and lost opportunities to exemplify excellence. Was my perception of Jenna changing? Did I overcompensate in my giving, doing good, and striving for excellence to cover her character flaws?

I did not want to be someone, nor settle for someone who has no comprehension of or little regard for excellence—a taker rather than a giver. I've known generally lazy people who, in times of need, become an overwhelming burden to others. I have experienced the unavailability of one who never runs out of excuses to help. I've worked with those who discount the need for excellence by not claiming tips and cash receipts or don't see a reason to tithe. They may very well own the most popular book of all time, the Bible, but shelve it like any other rarely used resource. It is easy to start a task when emotions are running high from excitement about something. But as a person of integrity, I need to finish what I start, even when the job is difficult or others are not watching my efforts, tracking my progress, or noticing my accomplishments.

As a person of excellence, I need to live by conviction, not compromise. If I want blessings and freedom from my brokenness, I need to commit myself to God and His ways, being uncompromising (see 1 Kings 18:21). In Mark 4:18–19, the Bible warns against the many pitfalls of compromise. I have convictions that are immovable and unchangeable. They are unwavering regardless of payoff or what anyone might say. I know that if I compromise, I sacrifice a part of myself. I have a conviction about places I will not go or with whom I will go, and what kind of friends I hang out with or make a part of my life. I consider if I would want that person to influence my future spouse. Godly character is not something I can compromise. I don't know who may be watching. Will those unseen observers see me as a compromiser or as a person of distinction?

Excellence Isn't Judgmental

I recently shopped at Target. I walked up to the checkout aisle with a small, one-dollar item in hand. I placed it on the rubber conveyor belt, making room for the person behind me. In front of me was a woman with a grocery cart full of items and more on the conveyor. As the person before her paid the cashier, I waited in curiosity, wondering if this woman was a person of excellence. I spent the next several minutes watching as the woman before me had item after item rung up. Not displaying a care in the world nor a glance my way to acknowledge insignificant me, she continued to pile up more purchases in front of my one little item. Feeling a little invisible and sensing my self-worth shrinking and shriveling away, I immediately knew God was giving me one last grueling story for this chapter.

As I watched this suffocating cocoon trap scene unfold in what seemed like a slow-motion test of patience, I recalled being in her shoes. I thought of all the times someone behind me had only two or three items in hand and how I insisted they go before me. I thought of the stranger whose bill I had paid when they did not have enough. God sees everything. He sees us doing the right thing even when it is hard.

The next time I was in Target, I found myself in the same aisle with one item thinking and wondering as before. The person in front of me turned around and hugged me. She was the lead singer and worship leader for one of the churches I attend. She was someone whom I asked to sing at my wedding with Jenna one day.

After I pondered that experience, I realized something startling when it came to excellence. If I wanted to be a person of distinction and excellence myself, I better stop judging people. A person of excellence does not judge others. I was expecting others to be at some level of self-denial equal to or better than mine. I was wrong. I am here to encourage and uplift others, not to look for faults in them. If you see anything beyond that in my writings, forgive me for my prideful attitude. Although I may detour from sharing every detail of my heartbreak over Jenna, my true intentions are to help others by sharing my story of brokenness.

Humility Is Excellent

While I probably thought of Jenna as humbler and more modest than myself, it was fascinating at times to watch her operate from behind the bar. She could have dressed in a way to attract much more attention from male patrons than she did, which I admired and appreciated as a brother in the Lord and potential suitor. Jenna being a part-time model, her humble habit of not getting all dolled up at Makara's was an excellent idiosyncrasy of modesty I respected. But, if she and I got the same shift, Makara and I would giggle in silence when Jenna would hyper-embellish the facts about her many varied career aspirations to customers while behind that bar. She was charming, captivating, and endearing, leaving the occasionally pompous me with a lot to live up to in the humility department.

A person of excellence is humble, so if I want to be a person of excellence, I must decrease and God must increase in my life. It is the same as what John the Baptist said about Jesus: "He must become more important, while I become less important" (John 3:30, CEV). It's not all that difficult to be a person of excellence if you are unselfish and humble. Since I'm not always that way, it requires some effort. The NASB 1995 version of Philippians 2:3–4 sums it up well: "… with humility of mind regard one another as more important than yourselves; do not merely look out for your own personal interests, but also for the interests of others." When I'm humble and regard others as more important than myself, I notice those in need.

I am usually aware of things I could do to make someone's day easier or their load lighter. I look for opportunities to put others before myself. Why? Because I appreciate it when someone does so for me. After going through my heartbreak over Jenna, I purposed to be a person of excellence as often as possible. It started to become a natural part of my life, like giving or doing good. It made me look for ways of doing things for a neighbor. It triggered me to remember others in prayer first and consider ways to help my friends. Excellence inspired me to prepare breakfast for Jenna, bring it to her in bed in her new guestroom, then wait for her to finish eating. Seeing her eyes light up was reward enough for my excellence in serving her. Sitting at the side of her bed, watching her enjoy the fragrant smell and zesty taste of what I had cooked, was pure pleasure for me. It seemed only natural to take her dishes for her and wash them before eating my meal standing in the kitchen.

Excellence with humility gave me the strength to respectfully bow down from an invitation I would have preferred to accept. After driving to Jenna's home, photographing her for her birthday, and taking some photos of her mom and sister, I took Jenna shopping and out to dinner in San Francisco. Upon returning, her parents had a birthday cake waiting. After a day of making it all about Jenna, I looked forward to the idea of spending quality bonding time with her family over a birthday cake.

But when her mom invited me to join them, Jenna interrupted with something to the effect of "Michael is tired and has a long drive home." Her phrasing might as well have been tantamount to the severest rebuke, even if not intended. I suppose I was tired, but the truth was that her best girlfriend was on her way over to share cake and candles. Jenna would have been torn between us and probably wanted to spend the time with her instead, so I humbly said, "Thank you," and bowed out without embarrassing Jenna. Still, it left a painful sting in my heart and seeds of doubt in my mind. Was my exclusion a sign that my value to Jenna was something she took for granted? Was it justified, or did being a person of excellence mean always assuming the best in everyone's intentions? Either way, it took prayer, along with what I had learned about worship and forgiveness, to conquer the rejection and sadness that flooded my eyes on the drive home that night. The virtual blood from my wounded ego left a crimson trail back to their kitchen table and red velvet cake with thirty candles.

Excellence Is Testable

My desire for excellence developed out of experiences and repeated nudging from the Holy Spirit for me to include it in this book. Excellence, like humility and morality, does not happen by accident. It's a real moral virtue you develop and achieve. The definition of excellence is "the quality of being outstanding or extremely good." But to me, distinction, nonjudgment, and humility in excellence are also like honesty and integrity. They are like peas in a pod, belonging together and going hand in hand. Integrity has a similar definition. It is "the quality of being honest and having strong moral principles." Integrity and honesty play vital roles in your life if you are a person of excellence. That role is so crucial that it needs an illustration within distinction.

So, I took the integrity test. I drew a stick figure on a sheet of paper representing the private me that no one but God and I saw. Next, I drew a circle around the stick figure, symbolizing the public me that others saw. The distance between the two represented my level of integrity. Then I asked myself, *How far is the circle from me in the real world?* and *Am I the same person in private that I portray in public?* I wanted to honestly know if I was posturing myself to personify an image I wanted others to see that may not be true, especially Jenna. The degree to which I was not who I represented was my standard of integrity, and that level of integrity influenced my ability to live a life of excellence. So the day I stopped adding updates to all my modeling websites was a start toward the right direction. I started making plans to take them down while still profitable and transform them into a Christian site, something that would be unheard of in my industry but close the gap between that circle and me, that stick figure.

I know people who pay lots of money to look good in person and online in the public eye, even when the facts tell otherwise. You might not recognize some of them without professional makeup and editing—I'm only half-joking. They pay for personal trainers, agents, and advisers. They go to great lengths to create a facade or an appearance of financial and career success—like a friend who brags about his income but makes payments on a car that retails for $100k more than mine and can only afford a studio apartment. The façade is as common as the cold but a complete anathema to those who know the reality. But for me, excellence acquired by honorable personal integrity was more valuable than money. The respect and admiration of others are better than anything wealth can offer: "A good name is more desirable than great riches; to be esteemed is better than silver or gold" (Proverbs 22:1, NIV). The Bible takes it a step further to proclaim it better to have little money and be honest than to be dishonest and rich: "Better is a poor man who walks in his integrity than a rich man who is crooked in his ways" (Proverbs 28:6, ESV). Moreover, if I wanted a faster recovery from my brokenness, then I needed to pursue practicing excellence. If you are curious like me, why not take your test today?

Excellence Is Learnable

The best parts of my life don't make it onto social media. My favorite photos of me and Jenna have never been seen by anyone but us. I've never even posted her best magazine covers or photos online. I also have never shared my path to excellence publicly until now. But I understand the reason why people feel the need to portray a particular image to others. The famous basketball coach John Wooden once said, "Be more concerned with your character than your reputation because your character is what you really are, while your reputation is merely what others think you are." When my pride replaced humility, or my boasting trumped praising others, I needed to consider excellence. Practicing excellence was something that set me apart from the crowd, and it was something I learned from a wise, inspirational leader.

I can hear Terri Savelle Foy's voice in my mind as I write. I had ingrained her words of wisdom into my heart through hundreds of hours of her video podcasts. As she said, "Excellence opens a door in your life that no man can shut. Excellence puts you on a path for success!" Excellence and integrity were prerequisites for where God wanted to take me in life. God wanted to bring me out of the pit of brokenness and into the promised land. If I lacked excellence and integrity, I would not reflect the real character of God in my life, leaving the door open for Satan to deceive me. I was giving the devil a foothold into my thinking by believing I would never move beyond despair. I didn't want to give him an inch because he would rob me of a mile.

If I ever wanted to be an ideal example, leader, or future suitor for Jenna, I would need to learn and study excellence. Doing so would reassure her family that their daughter had made a wise and acceptable choice. Her father's potential concerns about certain aspects of my photography business were something Jenna and I had discussed. Having shot and published models nude prior to meeting Jenna would not be something her father would look favorably upon, and rightly so. Removing such images from the internet and contemplating stepping aside from the glamorous life over every guy's dream, then writing about it, would be a first for someone in my line of work, but a necessary one. Learning and pursuing excellence was one step along the route to eliminating those things that were ungodly from my life that would block the path of a potential father-in-law's seal of approval. Learning about excellence was part of God's course of preparation for what was to come.

I've heard it said that what is next in your life is always connected to what is now. Was my breakthrough not coming to fruition because I lacked excellence in some unseen area? God noticed all the little things in my life. He observed if I picked up trash off the floor or put things back where they belonged rather than leaving it up to others. To my astonishment, I have seen firsthand people drop items on the floor and not hang them back up. It's discouraging, but nothing surprises me anymore. It reveals self-centered laziness in people rather than integrity. God is watching how we handle what some consider insignificant, small things in life.

The opening verse of this chapter tells what excellence did for Daniel. It made him distinguished and successful, commanding enormous respect. It brought him preference, power, and influence. It elevated him from being a slave, a nobody, to a high position in the kingdom under Darius, the ruler of Babylon from 538–536 BC. It put Daniel in charge of all the king's financial affairs and over 120 princes and three presidents. Why? Because God's favor was on him. And why was God's favor on Daniel? Because he had an excellent spirit. What did I learn from Daniel's story? It demonstrates that my standard of excellence can pave the way to my success. It attests to the critical role excellence plays in freedom from brokenness.

Honesty Is Excellent

Excellence and integrity had a lot to do with how honest I was when others were not watching. Excellence also required honesty through everyday personal interactions and never feigning sympathy or coming off as smarmy through my pain. A straightforward life is one that is free from deceit while being truthful and sincere.

If I lacked integrity, then honesty and reliability would be difficult. Being honest is something I worked hard at to have freedom from brokenness. Successful relationships with others required me to live an honest life. For God to bless my life, honesty needed to be a way of life for me because God's blessings are on those who live by truthful words and actions. "The LORD detests lying lips, but he delights in people who are trustworthy" (Proverbs 12:22, NIV).

As a broken person suffering through despair, every moment was a struggle to make it through the day. The last thing I needed was something to compound the problem or make it worse. So I looked at what God says about telling the truth: "Whoever would love life and see good days must keep their tongue from evil and their lips from deceitful speech" (1 Peter 3:10, NIV). The Bible also says that there are six things the Lord hates, seven that are detestable to Him. A lying tongue is number two on the list, according to Proverbs 6:17. Many people I have met are comfortable lying. I wish this were not so, but it is the truth.

In our culture, we often treat lying as something harmless. Many people even lie without a second thought. Much of the time, they may not even be aware when they are not being honest. They may exaggerate, changing the facts a little to make themselves look good. They might tell a police officer they didn't realize they were speeding or may cheat on their taxes. Why? If you had $100 in your pocket and found $1 on the ground, wouldn't you pick it up? That's why people cheat. They may make up stories about their past or file a false insurance claim. It is easy to think that a little lie is harmless. Before they know it, they may become more comfortable lying so that it becomes a habit. If you want to become a person of excellence whom God blesses, practice telling the truth daily.

CHAPTER 13: EXCELLENCE

I recall a day, years ago, when I pulled into the service department of my car dealership. It was a chilly day, and the service attendant noticed that my car heater was not working and had a solution.

"I can fix that for you!" he exclaimed. "You're only a little over the mileage limit on the warranty, but we don't have to mention that. No one will ever know. That way, you can have the work done for free rather than spending over $1,000 to fix it."

To his surprise, I turned down the offer. He asked, "Are you sure?"

Without hesitation, I responded with "yes." I knew that no one would ever know or care, but God would know. And now that the car no longer runs, you can only guess how much peace of mind I have in the decision I made years ago.

One of the most important ethical guidelines for many people is, "If you don't get caught, it's okay." The second is, "If you get caught, deny it." God looks at things differently. "You shall not steal, nor deal falsely, nor lie to one another" (Leviticus 19:11, NASB). Even if no one caught me doing something wrong or dishonest, God wanted me to tell the truth. After all, God knows the truth. No one likes or trusts a liar, cheat, or thief, but everyone loves and respects a person of excellence. So I strive to live with honest integrity, as God intended, and enjoy His blessings for it.

One of those blessings has been the trust and respect I have earned from Jenna, knowing only truth comes out of my mouth to her. She does not worry about an unkept promise or false hope I may have given her, for there are none. She does not doubt my loyalty or faith in her. Given that my business has exposed me to many facets of dishonesty and lack of integrity, it is unique that our relationship has steadfastly endured the honesty test of time, at least from one side of the table. From my vantage point, honesty is excellent, for it has removed a fear many women face with men.

What Matters Most

Growing up, I embraced the assumption that God does not punish good people. So I was kind, moral, ethical, virtuous, and honest before I ever pursued excellence. I was never an altar boy or boy scout. I never won prom king or queen, "most popular," or "best all-around" like my high school girlfriend, but I was a good boy. Growing up Catholic, I tried to keep the Ten Commandments, pray the rosary, and say the Hail Mary every day. My mom took me to church each week, kept the Sabbath, probably tithed precisely 10 percent, and never cheated on her taxes. As an adult, I didn't pray five times a day facing east or memorize the Torah, but I stayed sober and did good deeds for the most part. I could have supported MADD, joined PETA and Greenpeace, or given to the Red Cross and the Salvation Army while feeding the homeless. I could have become an Olympic medalist or won the Nobel Peace Prize. I could have been awarded that honorary doctorate or made the cover of Forbes Magazine.

I could have done all these things along with any other long list of platitudes, and where would it have got me? Nowhere! Salvation is not something we can earn. It is not a merit badge I could achieve or a test I could pass. No one could tell me how good I had to be to enter the kingdom of Heaven and earn eternal life after I died. You either have it or you don't. "Good people don't go to Heaven anyway—perfect people do," says Lead Pastor Chad Moore of Sun Valley Church in Arizona. So, how do we get perfection? Religion demands I earn it. But no one can achieve perfection—certainly not me. "We receive Jesus," Chad adds. It's a gift from God through Jesus Christ. And it was my choice to accept and receive it or not: "For by grace you have been saved through faith; and that not of yourselves, it is the gift of God; not as a result of works, so that no one may boast" (Ephesians 2:8–9, NASB1995).

Jesus didn't die so that I could have a religion or an excellent life. He died so I could have a relationship with Him. I pursue excellence to let the weight of brokenness lift from my chest. I know it will lighten my load and loosen my chains. I seek excellence for integrity's sake, character building, and self-respect. To recapitulate, I strive for excellence because little things matter. I seek it because it's distinctive, honest, learnable, testable, and nonjudgmental. But I do not seek it as a means to earn eternal life. I don't confuse living this way with God's path to salvation or for honor from others. I live a life of excellence to please God and not people. Because of this, God has healed my brokenness.

> "Whatever you do, work heartily, as for the Lord and not for men" (Colossians 3:23, ESV).

CHAPTER 14: KIRA

"Now listen, you who say, 'Today or tomorrow we will go to this or that city, spend a year there, carry on business and make money.' Why, you do not even know what will happen tomorrow. What is your life? You are a mist that appears for a little while and then vanishes" (James 4:13–14, NIV).

After Aslan's final *meow*, Kira remained my constant and ever-so-loving needy companion. She did not leave my side for the first two nights following his sudden death, for the sagging sadness out of nowhere just waylaid her. Tucked under my left arm, we mourned together over what the future would bring as a family of two now. Every night after, our bonding included repeated petting, talking, and snuggling in my attempt to comfort the tenderest part of her little brain. I was always mindful of her moans and meows, never knowing how long I had until they would end in silence. Like her brother, she was a joy I thanked God for in every prayer. Her adorable personality resurrected my memory's landscape of precious diamonds found in Aslan's presence and then lost.

Concern for Kira

Then came the day of concern for Kira. It was early May, five months after Aslan's departure. She came to me in bed late at night and in the early morning. Her meows were more like a scream for help than a greeting. She was fine when I pet her face but pulled away both times when I tried to pet her back, like she was in pain or fearful. Her tail was up and looked bent at the end as well. She skirted from my room to another, hiding, and as I saw her and called for her, she howled. It was clear that she was in pain and fear. She hid behind my bed in silence, and I saw her climbing on the love seat in an attempt to then crawl under it. I called her by name again. She looked back at me terrified, elevating on her tiptoes, and darted back down behind my bed again. That was weird and disheartening. Behind my king-size bed was her safe place. I called her in a soft voice, to no response.

She had been fine when I left to work for Makara the day prior. It was a routine for her to be all over me, lying on me or on my arm and purring. This morning, she was elusive and scared. It was almost like something happened between when I was gone the night before and sunrise. My sister said to leave her alone; she may be sick. When cats know something is wrong, they like to be alone and undisturbed. I thought she might be dying. Worry crept over me. Was my final chapter Kira's final chapter? The book was getting close to completion. She was my only company without Jenna visiting and staying in the guestroom. Other than the occasional client that hired me, my home was empty but for Kira and me. Without Kira, it would be me alone. This morning was the first since Aslan died that she did not come to me. Still, I will proclaim the name of Jesus because that is who I turn to in times of trouble, for He is in control and consistently shows up.

As I read my Bible, I opened to where I had left off the previous day. I had been reading through the Bible daily, starting with Genesis a few months earlier. This particular morning was quite interesting because I happened to arrive at Psalm 23. It was no coincidence, for by now, you know I do not believe in coincidences. "Even though I walk through the valley of the shadow of death, I will fear no evil, for you are with me; your rod and your staff, they comfort me" (Psalm 23:4, ESV). God was with me at this moment, only five months after Aslan said goodbye. "Surely goodness and mercy shall follow me all the days of my life" (Psalm 23:6, ESV). I had to trust God that this may be her time, being so old, because there was no way to take her to the vet with her sharp claws and frantic personality. I had never been able to pick her up for longer than a few seconds.

The twenty-third psalm, written by David, is comforting. It is a place of rest, where God guides, shields, and restores. I could interpret that to mean that God takes me from a place of brokenness to starting over again fresh. Amid my brokenness, He renewed my spirit and strength. God wanted to restore me to a place where I was before this all happened, as if it didn't. He wanted to bring me to a place of restitution in life for what I had suffered. I became closer to Him in the process so I could carry out God's plan for my life. Someday I will walk through the valley of the shadow of death knowing that God will comfort and guide me to a place of rest, for Jesus promised to always be with me.

Sounds of Silence

The next day I awoke to the emptiness of no cuddling cat at my side or feet and no response to my calls to her name. Fifteen years of my two pets being there daily and five months of the one that remained alone are memories. How quickly time passes. In the last few days, Kira had been doing something she had never done. She would sit on my stomach or chest in bed both morning and night. Her cry in a loud voice would end only by me petting her face and whiskers. She would, in turn, purr and lick my palms. If my hands left her face or touched her body instead, the loud meows would return. It would take quite a few minutes for her to settle down. She would then snuggle under my left arm, her usual routine since being a kitten.

You should take this very moment to cuddle and pet your animal or tell your loved one how much they mean to you. It is all over in the blink of an eye. When it does end, you will wish you spent more time with them, like I now do. You may think of the old song I recall at this moment. Simon & Garfunkel were not prophets, but some of their music, like "The Sound of Silence," pierced hearts. The lyrics transcended beyond their generation.

Day three found Kira motionless, tucked under my bedroom sofa, hidden from sight all day. I did everything I could think of, trying to make her feel better physically and emotionally—much like I had done with Jenna when she needed comfort. My calls to her went unanswered in silence, except for one soft meow late in the afternoon. Four close friends told me they were praying for her. Make no mistake: Jesus meets darkness with light. I saw it firsthand when I sat on the floor while reading and talking in a gentle voice to Kira. Then a real miracle happened. She crawled out from under the couch as if nothing had happened and started eating. I could hardly believe it. She let me pet her and even spent a few hours on my bed relaxing. She had lost weight during her three days of isolation, but her appetite was quick to return. The pungent smell from opening a can of tuna or grilling fresh chicken brought her downstairs rapidly. It was faster than the call of invitation. Within a few days, she was spending hours with me downstairs. When I would turn on the music to worship before bedtime prayer, I could feel her whisk by my feet in the dark. She wanted to be my plus one, my sidekick, like she and Aslan used to do together. It would not matter if it was 11 p.m. or 2 a.m.; she was there seeking my hand. Every miracle in the Bible first started as a problem. The same was true for Kira's revival from illness and perhaps the message in this book.

Three-Month Transformation

Only one significant change occurred after Kira's close brush with the hereafter. She spent more time with me during her awake hours, but the days of cuddling in bed morning and night were over. She slept under the sofa in my room instead. She spent more and more time in Aslan's old space in the guest room as well. It was like she had lost the memory of our routine. Contemplating what was up, I concluded that God's miracle was only preparation. It was a small deliverance. He gave me her for a while longer, but I needed to get used to enjoying her out of bed. I accepted this compromise, for it would make full separation less painful one day. To make a long story short, after three months, Kira was, to my shock, suddenly back to her old self. She was sleeping and cuddling in bed with me at night and visiting me during the day. She often called on me for attention from atop the stairs or from my room. I loved that adorable sound.

"Blessed are those who mourn, for they shall be comforted" (Matthew 5:4, NASB1995).

After a few months without her brother around, Kira became more attached, affectionate, and dependent on me. She would wrestle with her squeaky toy, swipe at her yellow Sharpie, or tug on her hair ties and expect me to roll them in her direction when they bounced away from her. Every day Kira would meow and howl from atop the staircase until I came up to pet and hold her. She was like an adorable little child wanting her daddy's attention. Her gurgled purrs, twirls, and brushes against me were akin to a child on the way to Disneyland. If she was cold, she would howl until I ran upstairs only to find her sitting in front of the space heater waiting for me to turn it on, then immediately quiet down. Often as I showered, she would come into the bathroom, press her nose right up to the glass door only to meow repeatedly for me to hurry up and finish so she could lap up the cool freshwater of the shower floor. When it was feeding time, her yowling and varied menu preferences were like an entitled chubby kid demanding frosting on a Snickers bar—I cherished every vocal outburst with a smile. It all became one more reminder of God's steadfast love for me. He loves me and wants my attention and dependence on Him like my cat loved and wanted the same from me. So hug your animal as a reminder that God loves you, too.

Déjà Vu Flight

As I wrap up this story in flight to Arizona, I trust God that Kira will be okay for a couple of days in my absence. I then realize there is a mother with her six-month-old in her lap to my right. The only baby on the plane happens to be in the seat next to me. This experience was like *déjà vu* from when I wrote about Aslan while in flight in December. Then it hit me. This brief moment is another reminder that God knows the end of the story from the beginning. I lassoed those comforting thoughts, for Kira would go on to live several years longer than her brother. And no matter how many times she threw up on the carpet or wet the bed in her old age, I would move heaven and earth to comfort her. There was no question I loved her unconditionally, just like my Heavenly Father loves me. But at the time, I had no idea what would happen with Kira or Jenna. Then, to my surprise, right after finishing this final chapter, Jenna reached out. The call came shortly after my landing.

"I miss you. I miss our time together. I miss our friendship and feel insecure about it. I love you. I want to come to see you and stay in the guestroom for a few days so we can talk," and, "I want you to come over to my parents' for Mother's Day."

These were only some of the words spoken by the one who unwittingly inspired this book—the voice I treasured as much as Kira's. Someone once said, "If you love something, set it free. If it comes back to you, it was yours. If it doesn't, it was never yours in the first place." I concur with Shannon Bream, who stated in her book *Finding the Bright Side*, "I don't believe God gives us cookie-cutter lives that must follow a certain path. He has different assignments for all of us." My unique career path and pivot were far from typical, which led to an unexpected assignment—sharing how God can heal the brokenness that all of us experience in one way or another.

I agree with Kayleigh McEnany, author of *For Such a Time as This:* "The Savior that I know will guide you through life if you just let Him." My brokenness felt like a never-ending roller coaster ride of dour suffering, tantalizing truth, heartrending sorrow, and daunting romance. But God had a plan and purpose that were better than mine, proving I could trust Him. He will guide you and carry you through trials as He did for me if you let Him. I would not have wanted to know all its travails along the way prior. But in the end, a five-year journey with a prized model and a couple of cherished pets proved worth sharing.

> "'For I know the plans I have for you,' declares the LORD, 'plans to prosper you and not to harm you, plans to give you hope and a future'" (Jeremiah 29:11, NIV).

Conclusion

"Above all, love each other deeply, because love covers over a multitude of sins" (1 Peter 4:8, NIV).

As I mentioned prior, someone once said, "If you love something, set it free. If it comes back to you, it was yours. If it doesn't, it was never yours in the first place." With those prophetic words in mind, I give you one last demonstration of God's wisdom. Our conclusion comes from the words of the one most appropriate, the one who inspired this book. And it occurred at the most logical of places, the volunteer job for Makara while assisting the one whose position I saved for two years. While working together near the cash register, just inches apart, Jenna paused, faced me, and looked at me with her beautiful smile.

"Would you ever want to go on a boat cruise?" she asked, with all the pyrotechnics of those sparkling hazel eyes and her batting lashes inches from my face.

You can answer that one yourself. Yet my straightforward response of "yes," without much hesitation, appeared to be a pleasant surprise to her. Next to "Do you have feelings for me?" and "Let's just kiss," it was the easiest "yes" I'd said in five years. She then proceeded to tell me the reason.

"I was hoping you would join a couple of girlfriends and me on a cruise to Mexico for my birthday," she added.

Memorable moments at work led up to this request. Having had fun interacting at work, where she purposely bumped her *derrière* into mine behind the bar, playfully commenting how hard mine was, Jenna had worked her way back into my good graces with demonstrations of flirtation and affection. These moments rekindled thoughts of when we sat at a dimly lit table together in the back, where I gently held her arm and stroked her wrist with my fingers where she scratched herself. Her soft, frosty white skin felt silky smooth to the touch of my slow-moving fingertips. It made me recall the time we talked for an hour, with her complimenting my character, sharing her intimate ideas, and inquiring about my plans for the future while I was sitting on the patio one evening when business was slow. It pleased me to no end listening to her verbalize her admiration for me after asking about my plans. It brought to memory her gasps for a deep breath as she rose on her tiptoes, with a big smile and wide eyes, the first few times I handed her my wad of cash tips from a night of working the same shift. It reminded me of the hello hugs, sharing meals, and teaming up to make her tips bigger. The cruise was not the first or last such request.

Two months later, working together again, we decided to take a stroll down the street for a little gelato. It was the middle of our shift, and things were slow enough for us to take a break. Jenna told me this time she wanted me to go with her to Hawaii for her birthday. She also wanted me to go to LA with her for her fashion show. Jenna showed me pictures on her phone of the kind of car she would like me to get one day and purses she liked. She talked about when she might want to have a child in the future. On our walk back, while enjoying our matching amaretto treats, she pointed out a bench.

"That is where we had our first kiss!" she said, smiling.

CONCLUSION

"Not my best performance," I interjected, shyly staring into the distance.

"Aw, no, silly," she reassured me as I laughed.

A few days later, Jenna was driving me to a car dealership to test drive the exact model she had recommended for me. Along the way, she made it a point to verbally express how aroused a car like that would get her. I had an immediate audacious response of my own to that bold and unexpected outburst of intimate flirtation.

"Well then, I guess you'll be needing that 3.5–4.0 carat princess cut diamond with a yellow gold band," I stated, looking out the passenger seat window with a confident straight face.

I had just repeated her own words back to her from two years prior, when she told me the kind of engagement ring she wanted one day. I did not see her reaction, but I wish I had held her hand when I spoke those words to her and asked her to pull over so I could kiss her. She was opening a door of affection toward me, and I was too much the reserved gentleman, having gone through mountains of history together.

My friends, family, and clients might be shocked at first, but I was ready to take the plunge down the aisle of permanent commitment and devotion, which were more desirable super-sized menu items for me than a short respite from singleness. Yet no final decision or monumental breakthrough came in either the birthday or ring conversations. But it is an excellent place to end. For the conclusion of our story, you'll have to read my next book. The only thing I can tell you is that I finished this book on the day of her birthday, not one of the other 364 days in the year. I don't know what that tells you, but it speaks volumes into my wheelhouse of understanding. As I have already written and remind you one last time now, God knows the end of our story from the beginning. Nothing is by chance; there are no coincidences.

Later, I found out something interesting about the location of that bench where Jenna and I had our first kiss. Makara informed me that she had met her husband at that location years earlier. Again, nothing happens by chance, and nothing is a surprise to God. He orchestrates our circumstances. As I write, I do not even know the end of our story, but I know the one who does. And He isn't telling, so neither am I yet. All that is important for you to know now is that God has a plan for you and me, and it is a good one! It is a plan that includes freedom from all our despair, sorrow, loneliness, and brokenness.

My story is not over, so I ask you to hold on with me, clinging to all the things I have shared that I learned about suffering from God's perspective. God loves you and me, and receiving that love is our healing medicine. I needed to commit to trusting God's Word of hope—a precept that freed me from bondage. My level of trust in our Lord to free me from worry, loneliness, and the pain of betrayal had to increase, for all my suffering had a purpose. Hopefully, you will trust God and do good until your breakthrough, and one day say, like me, "Now I get it."

I replaced worry with worship. It gave me the comfort and strength to endure. My dedication to regular prayer and forgiveness provided me with peace of mind and rest for my weary bones. I needed my doing good and giving to be exceeded only by my excellence and trust in God. For it is He who is more than able to do all that I could dare to ask. It will bring me a reward and favor. Trusting in God's power and doing good while resisting the temptation to try to control my situation became my new goal and a priceless boon. I purposed to be the kind of person my future spouse will admire. The benefits of using wisdom in my choices as a single person are many.

I encourage you to do these things, too, because the Lord, Adonai, listens to our heart's desires when we are suffering, remaining mindful of them even when His answers aren't what we prayed for and anguished over. Nothing about you or your situation is a surprise to God, for He is Elohim—the creator who formed you in your mother's womb and knew every word out of your mouth before you spoke. He strengthens our hearts while turning our tears to praise and joy. God will bring good to you, as He has done for me, for waiting on His timing. He will be close to you and heal your brokenhearted wounds, for He is Rapha—the healer. The Lord will rescue your crushed spirit and replace your broken condition with a double reward for all that you have suffered. He will supply all your needs, for He is Jireh—the God who provides. God loves you and can lead you to the right choices and an ideal mate, or He can restore your marriage, for He is the God of second chances. He will give you beauty for your ashes and never tire of loving, blessing, and strengthening you, for He is El Shaddai—God all-sufficient. He will exchange your former shame with honor and give you compensation for your suffering. God will make a way when there seems to be no way, for He is Yahweh—the great "I am," master of the universe.

Thank you for letting me share part of my story with you. I've given only one woman the key to my home and heart because only she had access to break it. I've also given only one woman my credit card to take out of the country to use as she wanted. And I've turned the story of that one woman into a book about our journey. And I finally selected the perfect song, "Growing Old With You" by Restless Road (you know, real edgy stuff that's not too schmaltzy), to play for her on my guitar after many requests (warning—plot twist!). Yet you might not expect this life-transforming statement: I am letting her go if that is God's will. I suppose prioritizing her honored the senses, but loving her had consequences. And you thought you were reading a photographer's memoir about his infatuation with a prized model who broke his heart.

What you were actually reading was a love story used by God to develop character in me through heartbreak and reveal the cure for brokenness to others. You should not presume that this story has a happy fairytale ending like "Beauty and the Beast." Cinderella has lost her glass slipper with all its splendor, and her Prince Charming is not looking for its rightful wearer. He won't unless God directs otherwise—for not long after we walked down memory bench lane, my confidante and soulmate, who trusted me with her most profound and private gut-wrenching tragedies, betrayed me once again, as I discovered on social media for a second time—leaving me dumbfounded, slack-jawed, and stunned in utter disbelief. "Whoever would foster love covers over an offense, but whoever repeats the matter separates close friends" (Proverbs 17:9, NIV).

Is it possible for disrespect and repeated betrayal to scream unthinkable so loudly that the victim loses any remaining respect and interest in the one once thought of as irreplaceable? Did God orchestrate these events to prepare us for or protect us from each other? Once again, I'd have to trust Him to guide me around the obstacles, for there was no clear-cut path. The truth is that I had my eyes set on the wrong prize. I was desperate to win Jenna's heart, hoping she would conclude that I was her best option, making her my idol. But in the end, I learned that only the Lord is worthy of my worship, for He alone holds the keys that unlock the chains to freedom from brokenness. In all His marvelous prescience, God can take what the enemy meant for evil and turn it into good (see Genesis 50:20).

And, "Sometimes God allows our hearts to break open in our sorrow so that He can pour more blessings inside," writes Shannon Bream in *The Love Stories of the Bible Speak*.

The ending to this love story had a different conclusion than I expected. Jenna got married in 2023, on the anniversary of our Ariana Grande date, days after burying Kira next to her brother after eighteen years of sleeping under my arm, and during the same week, our favorite restaurant was torn down and replaced by another Lazy Dog, the restaurant where we first met. You can't make this stuff up. We all like to think we are keepers of our own timetable when timing is precisely what rests in God's hands.

I admit my life hasn't worked out according to my plan. And you didn't need to read a mystery memoir to realize your life is an enigma to you. We don't have a clue what's around the corner, let alone five years from now. But that doesn't mean our lives are not out of control, for they are under the careful administration of the author of it all.

I hope you will continue your journey with me in my next book. It's hard to turn the page when you know someone whose eyes made time stand still might not be in the next chapter, but the story must go on. As a prisoner of hope, I know God has a good plan for the future when there is much more to reveal and unexpected things to come.

> "I make known the end from the beginning, from ancient times, what is still to come" (Isaiah 46:10, NIV).

Milton Keynes UK
Ingram Content Group UK Ltd.
UKHW031617231124
451036UK00003B/35